POLE

Moscow 4110

O c e a n

Pt.Barrow

Arctic Circle

Norman

Mackenzie

C A N A D A

3260

2780

Hudson Bay

ago

Edmonton

Yukon

Fairbanks

Nome

Matanuska

Juneau

1530

U. S. A.

Anchorage

Seward

Sitka

Ketchikan

Sea

Gulf of Alaska

1950

Seattle

Kodiak

1010

1950

Dutch Harbor

Is.

San Francisco

O c e a n

2400

1320

Hawaiian Islands

Honolulu

Richard Edes Harrison 1942.

ALASKA UNDER ARMS

THE MACMILLAN COMPANY
NEW YORK · BOSTON · CHICAGO
DALLAS · ATLANTA · SAN FRANCISCO

MACMILLAN AND CO., LIMITED
LONDON · BOMBAY · CALCUTTA
MADRAS · MELBOURNE

THE MACMILLAN COMPANY
OF CANADA, LIMITED
TORONTO

Alaska Under Arms

by JEAN POTTER

Endpaper by Richard Edes Harrison

New York
THE MACMILLAN COMPANY
1942

To DUSTY *and* HAROLD
and Their Comrades *in* Arms *in the* North Pacific

We're the fighting men of Kodiak,
We'll stand when others fall,
We're brothers to the eagle
And the wolf cry is our call.
The mighty bear's our ally
And the mountains and the sea
Stand with us in our vigil
To keep our country free.*

* From "Fighting Men of Kodiak," by Captain Roy D. Craft. Reprinted by permission of the Kodiak *Bear*.

PREFACE

THE DAY I finished this book, the Japanese attacked the Aleutian Islands.

People all over the United States began asking: "What have we got up there, anyway? What kind of country is it to fight in? to live in? What kind of people are the Alaskans? What does Alaska need from us, and how can we use it to help win the war?"

Alaska has been called "the most wonderfully misunderstood country in the world." Before I visited it on assignment for *Fortune* magazine, I knew as little about it as most Americans. This book is a reporter's account, based on intensive interviews with the people who are making the Territory's current history. Whatever value it may have comes from the fact that I went there for the purpose of finding out what Alaska really is like today, and what it offers to the nation that holds it in peace or war.

I saw men working hard to fortify the region, racing against time to prepare for the battles to come. I saw new bases taking shape on wilderness sites, and learned that the pioneer job of building those bases was one of the most difficult the Army and Navy had ever faced. I found that the Alaskans are alert patriotic Americans, with a peculiar frontier psychology all their own. I learned that Alaska is changing fast under the impact of the military program; that its whole economic and social pattern is bound to be reshaped; that the Territory, after long years of neglect, is coming into its own under the pressure of war.

As the Territory becomes a battlefield, many things change

focus, and a critical discussion of its problems may seem inappropriate to the hour. Yet the past era of well-meaning planlessness has produced many of the difficulties now faced by Alaska under fire. This is a people's war, and it is therefore vitally important that the American people have a realistic understanding of these problems, based on first-hand accounts, in order to give fullest support to all the steps which our Government may now take to use Alaska's strategic value in the war. I hope this book may make some contribution to that understanding.

While the interpretations contained herein are solely my own, they are based on facts and judgments given me by the men who know Alaska best; by government officials who are running the Territory's affairs, by Army and Navy officers, and by ordinary people—pilots, miners, merchants, fishermen, trappers and farmers—who are making their living in Alaska and preparing to fight there if necessary.

I owe many thanks to the people in Alaska who were so generous with their time and with their warm northern hospitality.

I am grateful to *Fortune* magazine for giving me the opportunity to see Alaska at first hand, and for making it possible for me to gather the material contained in this book.

I am also indebted to Joseph Kastner and Wilfred Goding for reading and suggestion, and to Gertrude Anne Edwards for remarkable feats in deciphering and typing the manuscript.

This book has been censored and approved by the proper authorities in Washington.

JEAN POTTER

New York City
July, 1942

CONTENTS

ALASKA UNDER ARMS

SLOW SHIPS AND FAST PLANES

LYING UP at the top of North America, Alaska has always seemed like a frozen waste, a continental dead end. It led nowhere, and, to most Americans, it seemed in itself a kind of nowhere. But this year Alaska suddenly came face-to-face with its destiny. Along its coasts, which are not remote, and across its far-stretched terrain, which is not ice-covered, the gravest and most far-reaching moves of war may be made. Alaska, fronting both on the shores of our closest enemy and on those of our most powerful ally, has become one of the focal points of the world war.

It is aviation that gives Alaska its chief value today. Yet the transport contradictions of this global conflict are especially sharp in the case of Alaska, for near as our northern possession lies, its power must be measured not only by the fast flights of bombers and fighters, but also by the tedious voyages of slow, crowded ships.

*   *   *

I went to Alaska, sailing aboard the weather-beaten *S.S. Mt. McKinley*, shortly before the United States entered the war. Even at that time the ship was under Navy orders, and going to Alaska was like going to a country at war.

As the old 400-foot triple-decker stood at Pier Two, Seattle, in the drizzling early morning fog, a long line of men shuffled up the gangplank. Welders, structural iron workers, carpenters, ditch-diggers, cat-operators—they were all going to report for work on the new Aleutian Navy base at Dutch Harbor. The whole boat was jammed with construction workers. The air was noisy with screeching and rumbling as longshoremen worked hastily along the dock, swinging supplies aboard.

The *Mt. McKinley* was late in sailing. We leaned, half asleep, along the rails of the narrow decks, shivering in the fog and blinking in the white glare of the lights along the pier. It was a dreary, confused scene. A drunk staggered back down the gangplank, and we watched him zigzagging back and forth among the piles of packing cases, waving his arms and shouting directions to the longshoremen.

"Powder monkey," said the man standing next to me. "Works with dynamite. They say they need him bad up there."

A uniformed steamship agent took the drunk by the elbow and led him solicitously up the plank. But soon he went tottering back down again.

When the assistant purser appeared, hoisting a sign reading "S.S. *Mt. McKinley* Sails at 12:00 Noon," most of us left the ship too and joined the milling crowds along the waterfront.

When we returned, hours later, longshoremen were still busy rattling back and forth on their handcars. Packing cases still towered high on the dock. The tackle was still noisily swinging supplies from shore to ship. There was no change in the scene, except that the powder monkey had fallen asleep against a wall, and a new sign had been hoisted reading: "S.S. *Mt. McKinley* Sails at 4:00 P.M."

For two years, I learned, Alaska-bound ships had been late in sailing. Even in normal times almost everything the undeveloped Territory needs has to be shipped up from the States. When construction was begun on our new northern bases, the Alaska Steamship Company was faced with a staggering job. Normally the line is busy in the summer salmon-canning season and slack in winter; but all during 1941 congestion was acute, for the line's small vessels were crammed with Navy cargo. Turning away thousands of tourists to make room for war workers, they steamed far beyond their regular routes, and all that year their erratic schedules were cause for profane jokes by travelers, pursers, quartermasters, and longshoremen alike. Long before the rest of the nation, Alaska became accustomed to the hectic confusion, the many changes and uncertainties of a country at war.

Some of the *Mt. McKinley* passengers, restless at the new delay, opened a bottle of whiskey. Others went down into the ship to try to get some sleep. They found that the small shabby cabins were still decked out with summer-cruise fixings; over each washbowl the neatly arranged folds of a red-lettered Alaska Line towel fanned upward from a tumbler, and in some of the rooms the stewards had placed baskets of fruit. But the double-decked bunks were hard, the boat shivered and shook, and the loud pulling and scraping of ropes and winches continued monotonously hour after hour after hour. Late in the afternoon the *Mt. McKinley* was still tied to the dock, workers were still leaning aimlessly against the deck rails in the fog, and longshoremen were still hoisting and hauling.

"If you don't get going in ten minutes," I heard one well-soused carpenter tell the purser, "I'll cancel my ticket. Who the hell wants to go up there, anyway?"

It was nearly dark when the *Mt. McKinley's* whistle sounded in a half-hour warning blast. With a surprising dis-play of festivity the purser began handing out packages of confetti. Some of the workers awkwardly hurled them down toward the dock, and two girls looking up at the ship began to cry. Only a few stragglers were there to shout goodbye as the hawsers were cast off and, with seagulls scattering around her gray hulk, the *Mt. McKinley* pulled out into the bay.

We crowded astern and watched the early lights blinking up and down the steep, foggy streets of Seattle. The *Mt. McKinley* started out past Bainbridge Island and soon began to pass along the spruce-fringed British Columbia fjords that she was to follow all the way north to Alaska.

Alaska is not far from the United States, but the trip through these spectacular, lonely fjords is like a voyage to a foreign land. Towering spruce-clad mountains hemmed in the ship as she cut her way through water as smooth as a lake, and all the first day, except for an occasional cannery or fishing boat, no sign of human life broke the wilderness. Up in the *Mt. McKinley's* social hall the men leaned back in comfortable chairs and looked out through big glass windows past the ship's bow, watching her course like spectators at a theater. Soon these men would be working overtime to build America's Aleutian outpost into a giant fortress, but that day they were relaxing like summer tourists. Other passengers, moving around the decks, wondered how soon they would see a glacier. Sometimes the *Mt. McKinley* passed so close to the wooded shore it seemed as if they could touch the trees. A Southerner in a lumberjack outfit went off to get his camera "in case we spot some big game." But the only signs of life were the circling gulls that followed the boat as she churned along her course.

When the meal chimes sounded along the companionways, we crowded below to sit at small tables behind bouquets of bright flowers. The menus, decorated with colorful paintings of Alaskan huskies, offered almost as many courses as those on an ocean liner. Beginning with India relish and celery *en branche*, we had our choice of fish, entrees, roasts, and salads, topped off with ladyfingers, candied figs, and *café noir*.

Early in the afternoon the men began to ask the purser when he was going to open the bar. They were disappointed to find that it was nothing but a kind of closet off a small, dingy dance hall. There were not many women aboard—only a few school teachers and Army and Navy wives, a prostitute, and a giggling two-hundred-and-fifty-pound redhead who had arranged her trip through a matrimonial bureau.

"I figure if that fellow don't want me," she told me, "another one will."

She knew what she was talking about—women are just as scarce in Alaska as they were on that boat. Even before the military preparations started, men far outnumbered women in the Territory. With soldiers and construction workers arriving by the thousands, the disproportion has increased and Alaska has become more and more completely a man's country; a soldier's country, a country of war.

After dinner the *Mt. McKinley's* violinists played for dancing, and everybody pitched in, including the mammoth redhead and the drunken powder monkey who told me he did not know "where the hell" he was going and did not "give a damn" anyway. The dance was a rugged affair, to say the least; and all night long couples strolled the darkened boat deck, looking up now and then to the brightly lighted American flag rippling in the wind above them. All night, as the ship moved northward through the dark wilderness, there were rounds of rowdy footsteps along the decks, and slamming doors, and popping bottles.

Next morning, when the passengers were awakened early by the foghorn, they could see nothing out of their portholes but thick, porridge-like gloom. The ship was moving more slowly. Steering his course through the narrow fog-bound channels, the Captain was navigating by the sound of the whistle's echo, much as he would measure underwater distances with a fathometer.

As I stood on the bridge watching the veteran skipper take his ship through the tortuous straits, his job looked difficult. Here and there red and yellow buoys bobbed in the smooth water to guide him on his course. At one of the narrows he stopped the ship's engines, and we had to wait an hour for high tide. The Alaska route is a notoriously treacherous one. As described by a Navy officer: "An Alaskan pilot is a mariner who knows not where the rocks are, but where they are not," and shipwrecks have been numerous.

In the years before the war program Alaska Steam, following its regular routes with skill and caution, operated without a passenger casualty. To veteran pilots the route is a challenge. An old timer who has learned its tricks is never quite content to run a ship anywhere else. However, green pilots fear it, and with good cause. In the past year several United States transports sank with their cargoes on the Alaska route and at least seven freighters ran on the rocks and were forced to return to port. Only a few months after our trip the *Mt. McKinley* herself was mysteriously wrecked off the Alaska coast and reported a "total loss."

I had, of course, no premonition of disaster, as I stood that morning on the bridge of the *Mt. McKinley*. But as the spruce trees and rocks loomed out of the fog in eerie, blurred shapes, as the blasts of the whistle continued hour after hour, as the lonely fjords stretched on and on, I was filled with a sense of gloom. I seemed to be going on an uncertain journey, to a desolate, remote land.

*   *   *

After completing my Alaska assignment, I returned to the States on a fast plane. Like the steamer, Pan American's big silver Lodestar was filled to capacity; for months the company has had to turn away two-thirds of its prospective passengers. It was just before noon that the three bells were sounded, and I climbed in with an FBI man, a Coast Guard officer, a lawyer, and a group of building contractors. There was frost on the windows as we roared across the Juneau field for the take-off, but it soon melted in the bright sunlight, and we looked out on a twisting pattern of barren rocky ridges, white snowcaps, and luminous blue-green glaciers along the spruce-fringed shore. Later the plane turned and flew inland. Dining on fried chicken, we gazed down on a frightening no-man's-land of bleak, unexplored, unnamed mountains that stretched off in all directions as far as we could see.

"Couldn't you land on one of those snowcaps if you had to?" I asked the co-pilot who had come back for a few minutes to chat.

"Lady," he said, "we don't figure on setting down anywhere around here."

We flew above this wilderness for hours, then circled and landed at the sleepy town of Prince George, British Columbia, where we chatted with Canadian airport officials and American Army fliers. Taking off again, we pursued our lonely route, and some of the passengers dozed off to sleep. They were short naps, however. Soon we saw the glittering roofs and smokestacks of Vancouver, and shortly afterward found ourselves coming down onto the runway of Boeing Field,

Seattle. The afternoon was still bright. It had taken us only five and a half hours to come down from Alaska to the States.

*   *   *

There is an ironic paradox about Alaskan transportation today. As the Pan American flights demonstrate, Alaska is no longer remote from the United States. It is a short run for commercial passenger planes, an even shorter one for bombers. As the plane flies, Alaska is also close to Japan, and it is no secret that our new northern bases are now the nearest ones on American soil from which an aerial blow can be struck at the enemy's homeland.

Yet there is no overland connection between the States and Alaska; no road or railroad by which those strategic bases can be supplied. Construction of a road up through Canada to Alaska was not begun until several months after the United States entered the war. Surveys for a possible railroad were also started, but it was feared that neither could be ready before 1943 at the earliest. In the meantime all heavy materials and supplies must go north through vulnerable waters, on slow crowded boats like the *Mt. McKinley*.

Nearly forty years ago the prophetic hunchback, Homer Lea, stated in *The Valor of Ignorance*: "As far as this Republic is concerned, Alaska is as insular as the Philippines, and sovereignty over it is determined by the same factors."

This thought was recently echoed by Anthony Dimond, the Territory's Delegate in Congress, when he declared: "Economically and strategically, the Territory is an island, as difficult to defend as a real island would be."

Slow ships and fast planes—these will settle the fate of our mammoth northern possession. They are at once its peril and its power.

II

BRIDGE TO ASIA

THE DEVELOPMENTS of the North Pacific war have been no surprise to the Alaskans. As they listened to reports of the historic Pearl Harbor raid, they heard a Tokyo announcer boast that Alaska, too, had been hit: that Dutch Harbor and Kodiak were in flames; that Sitka and Anchorage had been captured; that three thousand civilians had been killed in the bombing of Fairbanks alone. ·

That time, the claims were false; but knowing the relatively short distances of the North Pacific, Alaskans realized that their small frontier towns were under constant threat of attack. The first news of the war swept Alaska like a powerful electric shock, a far quicker and harder shock than that experienced in the States. There was good reason for this, for the Alaskans knew that their land lay closer than any other part of the American continent to Japan. The Japanese had long shown that they were aware of the Territory's strategic importance. Although the first enemy planes had bypassed the Territory, the Alaskans knew that their giant land with its steep, rugged shores and bleak islands might any day, any hour, become a theater of war.

When the first reports of the Hawaii attack came over the air on the fateful morning of December 7, Major General Simon Bolivar Buckner, head of the Alaska Defense Command, ordered a constant alert. Guns were fired at Fort Richardson, calling the men to arms. Soldiers at the fort were

9

rushed to fighting positions with ammunition in their belts. Fire guards got set. Planes took off. Army trucks with sirens dashed from the fort to nearby Anchorage to gather up the troops wandering around town. The wide streets were cleared of cars, and trucks roared through them with war supplies, hour after hour. Storekeepers began taping their windows. That night a total blackout was effected.

Early the following morning sirens shrieked and war planes thundered through the dark above the town. Frightened civilians, looking up through falling snow, soon realized that they were only American ships on patrol, but in the weeks that followed, the rumors persisted that enemy bombers and fighters had tried to fly in from sea that night; that a Japanese aircraft carrier had been brought across the Pacific to a point off the Alaska Peninsula, planning to strike at Alaska at the same time that Hawaii was attacked, but that a heavy sleet and fog had kept the enemy planes from bombing the bases.

Since December 7 there has been scarcely a flicker of light from dusk to dawn in towns near the Army and Navy bases. Wives and children of military personnel and construction workers were promptly evacuated to the States. Supplies of planes and troops were rushed north in increased quantities. Congress voted to send emergency food stores to Alaska, as well as to Hawaii and the other Pacific possessions. Home guards were formed in the towns. Authorities at some of the island bases advised civilians to dig themselves trench shelters in the ground near their homes. Even at Fairbanks, deep in the Interior region, each family was ordered to prepare a two weeks' bundle of food and clothing to carry into the hills at a moment's notice. News announcers at the Midnight Sun Broadcasting Company were cautioned by their employer to keep the excitement out of their voices. But the excitement was strong in their listeners' minds, and months before the Japanese struck at the Aleutians, Delegate Dimond told members of Congress: "My people feel they occupy a battlefield."

It took a war crisis to make most Americans aware of the unique, ocean-bridging location of our northern possession. Alaska lies up toward the top of the globe, where distances grow strange and foreshortened. It lies where the massive American and Asian continents nearly touch before they flow apart to edge the widening blue spaces of the Pacific. Far to the south, to get our convoys over to Australia, it has been necessary to move them slowly across seventy-five hundred miles of the world's greatest ocean. But up at Bering Strait, the Pacific is less than sixty miles across. The American and Russian Diomede Islands face each other across less than two miles of sea, and in the winter Eskimos have walked over the shifting ice in the space of a few hours. The Eskimos trade and visit back and forth. One of them, casually crossing over from the Russian side, recently flabbergasted the Army when he appeared with a group of American Eskimos for service at Fort Richardson.

Japan and Alaska are not so close as this, but they are still very much too close for comfort. For a thousand miles the smoking snowcapped volcanoes and bleak pinnacle rocks of the Aleutian Island chain front on ice-free waters, reaching out like a giant natural causeway almost to Asia. Attu, the farthest-out Aleutian Island, is nearer to Japan than to most of Alaska. The Aleutians are strung across the 180th meridian, the Fox and Andreanof Islands falling with America in the Far West, the Rat and Near Islands with Asia in the Far East. From Attu it is only 720 miles across the water to the

Japanese base at Paramushiro, only 600 miles to the Soviet base at Petropavlovsk.

The three countries are grouped closely around the waters of one sea, sharing much of the same weather; and history books, as well as maps, tell how short the distances are between them. Petropavlovsk was named for the *St. Peter* and *St. Paul,* rude boats in which a Russian expedition, led by Vitus Bering, set out to explore the North American Continent over two centuries ago. It was chiefly on the basis of their trips that Russia claimed ownership of Alaska. The Bering party encountered a fierce gale along the south shore of the Aleutians. They battled the same seventy-five-mile winds that Alaskan pilots and Army fliers today call "williwaws," the same dense fogs that are likely to play a crucial role in the North Pacific fighting. Petropavlovsk, like the Alaskan bases, is warmed by the Japan Current and is ice-free throughout the year. Unlike the waters along the Aleutians, the Sea of Okhotsk is ice-bound most of the year, but because of frequent thick fogs and ferocious gales, flying conditions there are similar to those along our island chain.

For years most Americans have thought the logical route to Asia lies past Hawaii, but this is by far the longest way. (From Seattle to Yokohama by way of Hawaii is 6,300 miles. By way of Alaska it is only 4,900.) The short (great circle) route from the northwestern part of the United States to the heart of Japan crosses the Aleutians twice, and Dutch Harbor is a thousand miles nearer than Pearl Harbor to Tokyo. (All distances in this book are given in statute miles.)

The Aleutians have been called the greatest chain of potential island bases in the world. The late Brigadier General William ("Billy") Mitchell, whose predictions on the crucial wartime importance of the airplane are now being validated, once declared: "The United States is in a better position than Japan to prosecute an offensive campaign by air. We own islands within striking distance of Japan's vitals. An aerial campaign against Japan could be pushed to best advantage from Alaskan air bases."

When I interviewed General Buckner at Alaska Defense Command headquarters shortly before the war began, this possibility appeared even then to be strong in his mind. Looking up at his wall map, which showed the Aleutians pointing ominously toward Asia, he told me: "The Alaska Defense Command is the wrong name. We should be called the Alaska *Offense* Command." Since the General made this statement, events have rendered the distinction even more important, the requirement for action more pressing. As islands to the south were conquered, Alaska became one of the few remaining points from which an offensive blow could be struck at the aggressor's homeland; at the fortified islands of the nearby Kurile chain, at Tokyo, at the munitions factories of Osaka, the shipyards of Yokohama, the naval bases of Sasebo, Kure, and Yokosuka. From the Aleutian Dutch Harbor base it is only 1,600 miles to the northernmost Japanese base at Paramushiro. After conferring with President Roosevelt early this year, Alaska's Governor told reporters: "We were thinking in terms of offensive warfare rather than of defensive warfare. It is the offensive that has to be bolstered."

The Japanese know, of course, that the Alaska threat is one that can be turned either way. They know that if they should take Hawaii they would still be 2,400 miles distant from the United States; but that if they could get possession of southeastern Alaska, only some 570 miles would separate them from our borders. It is less than four hours in a bomber from one of the south Alaskan bases to Seattle.

For years the Alaskans have felt uncomfortably close to Japan. They are used to picking up Tokyo broadcasts. Long before the war they heard reports of Japanese submarines operating off their shores. In the fall of 1939 five Indian fishermen saw an unmarked vessel with a periscope running close to southeastern Annette Island, and Delegate Dimond, after hearing their accounts of the episode, feels that it was, without question, an enemy submersible. A few months before the Japanese attack on Hawaii, Soviet fliers on their way from Siberia to Seattle sighted another unidentified submarine from their planes, and in the crowded bars of the Navy base town there were rumors of enemy subs running in nearby waters "thick as catfish." Rumors grow big in Alaska's small towns, but one thing is certain: for a long time Japanese fishing boats have come across the Pacific to sink their nets in the waters off Alaskan shores, and they have been doing a great deal more than fishing.

Ten years ago, the Japanese, having largely depleted the run of fish off their own shores, began to work off the coast of America from Mexico to Alaska. In 1932 they sent floating canneries across the Bering Sea and subsequently extended their trips into the Bristol Bay region, nearer Alaska's shore. A Japanese government boat was sent across for an extensive investigation of fisheries' possibilities along the Alaskan and Pacific coasts. In 1936 Japanese officials came to the United States to propose joint government surveys of the fish in waters off Alaska, and early the next year a brash Japanese fishing tycoon proposed to a group of West Coast packers that new fisheries in these waters be developed jointly by Japanese and American capital.

The two-fisted Alaskan fishermen of the Bristol Bay region were already thoroughly aroused against the steam-powered

Jap trawlers they were encountering in its lonely waters. The Jap boats, they reported, were using fake call letters. When sighted, they would move away at once and their radios would remain silent for several days thereafter. A salty old-timer, J. E. Shields, master of the *Sophie Christensen*, caused a sensation by demanding that Washington supply guns to drive off the intruders. Other fishermen were also in a fighting mood, and a group of them tried to persuade a Bristol Bay Air Service pilot to fly them over the Japanese ships so that they could smash them with homemade dynamite bombs. In 1937 the State Department lodged a protest with Tokyo and received "assurances" that the Bristol Bay fishing would cease. Japanese boats have not been sighted in Bristol Bay itself since that year; but only a half-year before the war broke out, Captain E. Jackson of the American freighter *Clevedon* encountered and photographed a fleet of eight large trawlers, headed by the *Kosei Maru* of Tokyo, in the Bering Sea off Nunivak Island. This fleet was also observed by fishermen from the Aleutian village of Dutch Harbor, where one of our three main Navy bases was under construction.

At that time they were moving well offshore from Dutch Harbor; but in earlier years Japanese boats ran close to the Aleutians, and it is feared that they know the waters along the strategic island chain at least as well as we do. Native Aleuts and the skippers of our government patrol boats have seen them "fishing" with lines marked off in fathoms, and have even found evidence of their landing on the bleak shores. Japanese newspapers and food cans have been found beside the dead ashes of campsites at important bays and inlets. Farther north on St. Lawrence Island a party of Fish and Wildlife Service officials, arriving on an inspection tour, were advised by the Eskimos that a group of Japs had been there the previous day, coming up close to the town of Gambell and trying to barter liquor for fur boots.

According to the account of Mrs. O. J. Murie, wife of one of the government officials:

About July 21, 1937, at Savoonga, St. Lawrence Island, Alaska, a Japanese ship which appeared in the binoculars to be a large freighter or floating cannery was sighted off the northeastern tip of St. Lawrence, heading west.

The next morning very early, our schooner, the *Trader,* anchored off Gambell, and the Eskimos told us that a big Jap ship had been offshore some distance, and two little vessels close inshore. They offered the Eskimos whiskey, beer or wine for fur boots, but the leader of the Eskimos told them that no liquor was allowed on the island and that they, the Japs, would get into trouble over that. The Jap captain then asked if there were any white people on the island and the Eskimos said, yes, the Government school teacher. (The teacher, Mr. Hinckley, had gone on a hike inland that day so was not aware of the ships till later.) The Jap captain then asked, "When do you expect the coast guard cutter?" The Eskimo leader said, "Any day now."

The Eskimos went ashore but planned to go out again. However, as soon as they were ashore, the Japs hoisted anchor and departed, and were out of sight when our party arrived.

Japanese espionage in Alaska has not been confined to the activities of fishing boats. By the last census there were 263 Japanese residents in the Territory, half of them foreign-born, and another 776 worked in the canneries during the summer salmon-fishing season. As soon as war began, an internment camp was established for the foreign-born residents, and they were later evacuated from the Territory. Some of those arrested had detailed topographical maps in their possession. Every Alaskan knows that the Japanese have conducted espionage activity in the Territory for an amazingly long time. More than twenty-five years ago, according to a first-hand account, residents of Cordova saw a mysterious light bobbing along the wilderness shore opposite their town. Taking a boat across the water they found a Jap carrying a lantern and followed him to a shack where they found detailed topographical maps and charts of the nearby waters. This was not last year, or the year before; it was a quarter of a century ago. Incidents of this kind give an inkling of the active interest the Japanese have long maintained in Alaska.

After the signing of the Rome-Berlin-Tokyo Pact (1940) Japanese espionage activities in Alaska took on a new and more threatening cast. According to the London-published weekly *Zeitung*, the Nazis have developed a comprehensive plan for attacking Alaska through Russian Siberia; and after the pact Captain Fritz Wiedemann, Adolf Hitler's former personal adjutant and former consul general in San Francisco, worked closely with Japanese agents in touch with spies masquerading as fishermen in Alaskan waters.

A sinister and little-known war background story also exists with regard to the White Russian colony in Juneau, and is especially alarming in view of the *Zeitung's* exposé. In the years following the Russian Revolution a group of exiles arrived in Juneau, many of them securing jobs at the gold mine. According to the report of an outstanding Alaskan, these men as long as ten years ago were in the habit of raising their vodka glasses at parties and drinking toasts "to 1942." When queried, they smiled and passed it off as a joke. Ten years ago, when a group of them came into a shop to buy a gift for Madame Tulinseff, leading member of the colony, they requested that 1942 be engraved on the back of it. Again, no explanation was given. "It's just a year," they told the storekeeper. A few months after the Pearl Harbor attack it was reported that government agents investigating one of these White Russians found correspondence with Nazis among his papers.

Although they thought little about it until recently, the Alaskans have long been aware of the existence of Nazi sympathizers in their midst, including not only several merchants of German birth or extraction but also one of the most prominent bankers in the Territory. More than once they have heard reports of the formation of Bundist groups, and they have also noted with suspicion the activities of occasional German "tourists." They also remember the statement of a Nazi author, Alfred Wollschlager (A. E. Johann), reprinted in *Alaska Life*, that "Alaska is only waiting for the advent of a people who are a match for her . . . Alaska is one of the great reserve territories of the Nordic race."

While foreign plots developed, Alaska remained a distant and barren iceberg in the minds of most Americans. The average man in the street knew little about the Territory and cared less. In spite of this, he complacently considered it a sort of preordained possession of the United States. The facts are quite otherwise. Although Alaska, geographically speaking, is a part of the North American continent, it has been a United States possession for only seventy-five years. For nearly twice as long, its history was linked to Asia. Officially discovered by Russian explorers in the early eighteenth century, Alaska was ruled under the Imperial flag until Congress voted to purchase it in 1867.

All through Alaska there are scattered remnants of the Russian occupation. The Navy base at Dutch Harbor is located near the site of the oldest Russian settlement in Alaska, established in 1760, and the base at Kodiak stands near the site of the first official Russian colony at Three Saints' Bay, established in 1784. Russian churches with fat bell-towers still stand amid the war activity of both these towns. Much of the social life of Juneau, Alaska's capital town, re-volves around the mirrored bar of the swanky little Baranof Hotel, named for the aggressive Siberian businessman who ruled Alaska for twenty years as director of the Russian Amer-ican Company. Alexander Baranof's portrait hangs today over the door of the hotel lobby, looking down almost cynically, it seems, on the confusion below: the ever present pile of suitcases, the busy Pan American agents, the periodic crowds of Army and Navy officers, salesmen, contractors, business-men, and Washington officials who gather to wait for their planes.

In the nearby town of Sitka, founded by the Russians as "New Archangel" in 1799, Baranof lived in a wooden "castle," ruling a vast part of America extending as far south as San Francisco. Sitka is today the site of a third major Alaskan Navy base, and there too, thousands of soldiers and sailors. look up to the green-domed tower of an ancient Russian church which commands the main street.

It was at Sitka, on October 18, 1867, that the Russian Imperial flag was lowered and the Stars and Stripes were raised over Alaska. Relations between Russia and America were unusually cordial, and those cordial relations were an important factor in our decision to purchase Alaska, although ambitions for empire also played their role. One reason for the purchase was our desire to accommodate the Russians, who had been losing grip on their Eastern dominion and pre-ferred to sell it to a friend, rather than to have it fall to a foe.

It was a complicated international situation that led to the Russian-American friendship of that day. On the verge of conflict with Britain and France over the Polish nobles' insurrection, Russia had dispatched her fleet to New York and San Francisco in order to get it where it would be less vulnerable and where it could be used against the enemy. The Civil War was then raging in America, and New Yorkers welcomed the fleet because they, too, were threatened by the British and French, who had shown sympathy to the Confederate cause. According to Gideon Welles, Secretary of the Navy, it was hoped that the Russian fleet's appearance in American harbors might "moderate" them.

There is a striking likeness between the friendly American-Russian entente that existed at the time of the Alaska purchase, and the wartime alliance of today. The enthusiasm caused by Molotov's recent visit to the States is an echo of the rejoicing that occurred when the Russian warships steamed into Long Island Sound nearly eighty years ago. According to the New York *Daily Tribune* of that time, "There was a spontaneous ebullition of good feeling on the part of the crowding and jostling people . . . a gala day in certain parts of the city." According to the *Zeitung*, this was easy to understand, in view of Russia's friendly alliance with America in "the terrible war into which Barbarism, even with its decrepitude, has been strong enough to plunge us."

"God bless the Russians," Gideon Welles wrote in his diary, expressing the same sentiment that millions of war-anxious Americans are feeling now.

Such relations as have existed between Alaska and the Soviet Union have been informal and friendly. When the Soviets began development of their gold-mining industry, they enlisted the help of several Alaskan engineers, including Jack Littlepage, who received the Order of Lenin in 1936 for his long years of service in Russia.

When Donald MacDonald, Alaskan engineer who first proposed the International Highway, wrote to Soviet highway officials, suggesting that they build a road to Bering Strait as part of their current five-year plan, this resulted in extensive technical correspondence between Mr. MacDonald and the Russians concerning ways and means of building roads in "the land of perpetual frost." Writing in June, 1931, the U.S.S.R. Chamber of Commerce for Western Trade told Mr. MacDonald: "Your project raised great interest among our organizations. But unfortunately, our country cannot face the problem of constructing highways to the Bering Straits as a practical one to be solved in the nearest future. Thus, for the nearest time to come, the linking up of the highway construction of Alaska with the transport system of the U.S.S.R. may only be realized by aviation which, of course, develops much quicker than highway construction. Although your daring idea of an automobile communication between our countries is far from being practically realized, we still hope that the already existing business relations between us will continue to our mutual interest."

On several occasions, Alaskan and Russian pilots have conducted joint searches for lost scientists and fliers, like motorists lending one another a hand on lonely country roads. The Russians helped in the search for Colonel Carl Ben Eielson, foremost Alaskan pilot, when he was killed in 1930, and in 1933 Jimmy Mattern was rescued by a Soviet plane piloted by Sigismund Levanevsky. Four years later, Mattern joined other American and Canadian fliers in their fruitless search for Levanevsky, who was lost in an attempted flight over the Pole. The Russians hired Alaskan planes to aid the scientific expedition led by Professor Otto Schmidt when the party was marooned on an ice floe. On this occasion relations became so cordial that the Soviet government presented the Order of Lenin to Bill Lavery and Clyde Armistead, of Fairbanks, who serviced the planes, and gave them each a life pension.

The occasion of the 1937 search for Levanevsky is the only time, up to the present war crisis, that organized weather reports from the numerous Siberian stations have been received in systematic fashion in Alaska. When reports from the Russian stations were gathered in Fairbanks in 1937 the chief of the United States Weather Bureau stated that there was a noticeable improvement in the accuracy of reports as far east as New York. However, after the search was concluded the cooperation ceased; and in this sense, too, the short space between the Asian and American continents remained unspanned.

Close as they lie, Soviet Siberia and American Alaska have had little direct contact with each other. There have been few efforts to cross the space between the two countries.

The outstanding attempt occurred shortly before the Alaska purchase, when Western Union spent three million dollars on the construction of a telegraph line to run up through Alaska and across Bering Strait to Russia. Several attempts to lay an Atlantic cable had failed, and accordingly the Pacific project was begun. An act was passed and signed by Abraham Lincoln in 1864 "to encourage and facilitate telegraphic communications between the eastern and western continents." Russian cooperation was obtained and poles were erected across the Alaskan and Siberian plains; but the project was abandoned when the cable was successfully laid across the Atlantic.

Another attempt at inter-continental connection by way of Alaska was made by E. H. Harriman, last of the great American railroad builders, who proposed construction of a railroad with a bridge or tunnel across the Bering Strait to Siberia; but this, too, failed of realization.

Alaskans have never known very much about the extent of military activity across the water in Siberia, and do not know much today. They know, of course, that the Soviets have large bases at Vladivostok, at Khabarovsk, and at Petropavlovsk, but where else they have built fortifications and installed troops, guns, and planes has remained a mystery. There have been occasional flurries of excitement in Alaska over reported Siberian fortification, but there has been little fear of Russia in the Territory. The emphasis in planning our Alaskan bases has been almost entirely anti-Japanese. One prominent Army officer in Alaska told me: "We never had very much fear about Russia. After all, she has a whole continent of Alaskas." Another remarked: "Fear of Russia? I should say not! Russia is the one thing that is holding our enemy."

Writing in the fall of 1941, Herbert Hilscher, editor of *Alaska Life,* leading Territorial magazine, declared:

At this writing no one knows whether Japan will join Hitler in his attack on Russia. But if the Japanese fascists can swing the deal at home, the Army and Navy of the Rising Sun will strike at Siberia . . .

All Alaskans and the U.S. Army and Navy know that if the flags of the Nazis and the Japanese fly over Siberia our position in the Northland will be extremely grave . . .

All that we in Alaska can hope for is that the Russian Bear can stop the march of Hitler and keep Japan from overrunning Siberia. Every day that Stalin, by might of force, can delay the Nazis gives our Army and Navy just that much more precious time to augment the defense of Alaska . . .

Alaska must be made into an arsenal of democracy. It must be made as impregnable a fortification as Gibraltar. For if Russia falls, who can say at what unannounced hour bombers, parachutists, and air-borne troops may not descend on Alaska?

Today, as the fate of all civilization rests on Russia's ability to beat back the Germans and as Russia is threatened with a Japanese attack in the East, Alaska occupies a uniquely strategic position. Although Alaska's proximity to Japan has appeared more significant to date, its proximity to Russia may command an equal amount of popular attention as the conflict develops. Bridging the Pacific at the top of the world, Alaska represents a great potential supply line for the United Nations. It is a giant bridge between the United States, their foremost arsenal, and the Soviet Union, to date their foremost fighting power.

Even before I sailed north from Seattle, I saw signs of friendly teamwork between the United States and the Soviet Union, and realized the potential importance of Alaska to both countries in the war. With other reporters I drove out to the Sand Point Naval Air Station to witness the arrival of two red-starred flying boats which had unexpectedly come down through Alaska, stopping off at Nome and Sitka. Out of these planes climbed forty-seven Russians (twice the ships' normal capacity), their clothes wrinkled from the cramped journey across the northern wilderness. Head of the delegation was Brigadier General Mikhail Gromov, who today heads a unit at the Soviet front. The Navy, receiving them officially, rushed them to the Olympic Hotel in two busses and banned photographs and interviews. Little was known about their mission. According to some reports the group consisted of technicians sent to inspect American aircraft plants; others said they were pilots, who had come to ferry war planes back to the Soviet fighting front.

Seattle reporters and photographers, after dolefully standing around the hotel lobby for several hours, finally gave up and went home.

Later in the evening, when I wandered into the hotel game room, I was surprised to find that a group of the Russian fliers had had the same idea first. Young and energetic, with close-cropped heads, they kept up a constant stream of talk and hearty laughter among themselves. They offered me some of their long, flat cigarettes and motioned me to show them how to play the pin-ball machine. However, they much preferred another game which involved firing an electric gun at a moving tank. Crowding around it, they took turns, cheering and groaning as the luck went. At first they were slow and over-precise; but when a Navy pilot standing beside us showed them a way to follow the tank across, they caught on fast, and some made excellent scores. The Navy man, who spoke Russian, had been delegated to entertain them.

"These kids have been around," he told me. "See the one that's playing now? He bombed Berlin."

For a moment I was almost dizzy with new realizations of geography. Since high school days I had visualized Alaska as a remote polar place, and Russia as a country lying across the Atlantic. Suddenly I realized that Alaska is the inside track to Russia; that the two big red-starred seaplanes, thundering over our northern Territory on their secret mission, were blazing a new route that might soon develop into a powerful line of aerial supply. Russia and the United States were not only allies, they were neighbors—joined through Alaska.

Few Americans realize the amazingly short distances of the far north. Few are aware of the transportation achievements that are opening up historic new routes across the top of the world. Yet they may play an important role in this war.

The most sensational development is the Northeast Passage which the Russians have pioneered around the top of Siberia all the way from the Pacific to ports like Archangel and Murmansk. Taking their freighters through by means of powerful icebreakers and ice-reconnoitering planes, the Russians began commercial use of the route in 1934. Today, according to a Soviet Embassy dispatch, "dozens of ships make it every year." From Seattle to Archangel by this route is only some 1,500 miles farther than the journey from Seattle to Vladivostok, and only half as far as the supply routes from America to Russia by way of Iran. The Soviet dispatch, commenting on the protection and shortness of the Northeast Passage, declared: "Exigencies of war have made clearer than ever the great value of this new transport route."

Spectacular aviation developments have also occurred in the far north in the last few years. At the end of 1941 the Soviet Embassy announced that Arctic aviation had increased 40 percent over the previous year and that a new 5,000-mile airline had begun service across northern Siberia from Moscow to Anadyr, which is only 380 miles from the Soviet East Cape air field. East Cape, in turn, is only 150 miles from the United States air base at Nome. It is a matter of public information that there are also large Soviet air fields down the Siberian Pacific coast, around the Sea of Okhotsk, and all the way to Vladivostok, and that fields also exist on the Kamchatka Peninsula with a regular air freight service operating inland from Petropavlovsk.

In the American northland historic aviation developments are also taking place. Two years ago Pan American Airways began regularly scheduled flights from Seattle to Alaska. As long as ten years ago the company bought an interest in an airline in Alaska with the hardheaded business plan of establishing a commercial route into Asia. It was with this incentive that it pioneered its Alaska operation and ran the

line for many years as a losing business. When the Civil
Aeronautics Administration began to develop the Alaskan
airways in 1939, it, too, was planning for a commercial route
through Alaska into Asia.

This CAA program was amplified as war threatened, and
a new chain of inland air fields was hastily constructed
through western Canada under the auspices of the Canadian-
American Joint Defense Board. Again, the northern distances
are astoundingly short. The trip from Chicago to Vladivostok by way of the new inland Canadian, Alaskan, and
Siberian air fields would be only 7,000 miles as compared
with nearly 12,000 miles by way of San Francisco and the
Philippines. It is not only the short way, but the only overland way to fly to Asia: planes flying this route avoid the vast
ocean distances to the south.

It is not generally realized that Alaska is double-pronged;
that the enormous, far-flung country provides two different
and widely separated ways of flying to Japan. These new
inland air fields, running north through Fairbanks and Nome,
represent one way to get there. The new Navy bases, spotted
out along the southern coast and Aleutian Island chain, represent another.

It is generally assumed that the Aleutian route is the short-
est one to Japan. This is true if you are flying from Seattle;
but if you are flying from Chicago, the Fairbanks-Nome-
Siberia route lying farther to the north is shorter. In either
case, the Russian air fields are spaced like stepping-stones
between the Alaskan bases and major objectives in Japan.
From the Aleutian base at Dutch Harbor it is some 2,800
miles to Tokyo; a thousand miles closer than Pearl Harbor,
but still a long way. From Dutch Harbor to the large Russian
base at Petropavlovsk, however, it is only 1,400 miles, and

from Petropavlovsk to Tokyo some 1,500. From Vladivostok to Tokyo it is only 670.

Today, as thundering war planes are cutting the short northern distances still shorter, national boundaries are also being effaced. The joint war plans of the United States and Canada to the south are connecting the whole Pacific Coast into one unified military area, and, by the simple facts of North Pacific geography, the fate of Alaska is inextricably bound up with that of Soviet Siberia.

One high-ranking Army officer told me: "Alaska is our front door to Japan; but Russia is the key."

Just when and how Alaska will come into full use as a bridge of war depends on so many factors, including the speed of our aircraft production and the progress of battle at far distant points throughout the world, that speculations written on this subject today will most certainly be obsolete tomorrow.

Weather will play a decisive role in the coming battle of the North Pacific. Dr. Vilhjalmur Stefansson, world-famed Arctic expert, stated in the June 15, 1941, New York *Herald Tribune*:

If the Japanese deliberately start a Siberian war, they will start it at the end of winter, when the ice which they fear has disappeared from the Asiatic coastline that trends southwesterly from Bering Strait past Kamchatka to the Sea of Okhotsk and to the waters of Sakhalin. The last of that ice disappears in June; the earliest seasonal date for a Japanese attack is therefore about now, if they think of the war as primarily between themselves and the Soviet Union in this sector.

The Soviets grasp their own winter superiority, and they know also the superstitions and other handicaps of the Japanese. So a war between these two countries, if started by the Soviets, would logically begin in November, when the rivers are everywhere bridged by ice, when the lakes are smooth fields for the advance of tanks and mechanized guns, when the swamps are no longer quicksand and bog and sticky mud but hard as concrete and fairly smooth.

No one can foretell the exact timing and the precise form of the coming struggle in this area, but in mid-July, 1942, one thing is clear: Alaska is one of the greatest potential offense bases in the hands of the United Nations. The time may well come when a large-scale offensive action, thrust out through Alaska, will be judged necessary to save the whole challenged free world.

III

A JOB BEGUN LATE

"ALASKA IS away off by itself. We do not know anything about Alaska."

This statement was made by Lieut. General Henry Arnold, Chief of the United States Army Air Corps, in the spring of 1939 as he stood before a Congressional committee seeking appropriations for an Army cold-weather experiment station at Fairbanks.

Our people have got to be trained how to fly up there [the General told members of Congress], about the weather up there, the kind of clothing they must have. How to start an engine when it's forty degrees below zero. How to keep the oil from congealing before you get it into the engine. What happens to a metal airplane when you bring it from this forty degrees below zero temperature and suddenly put it in a warm hangar. We have got indications and every reason to believe that the rivets just pop out. All these things we have got to go through, and there is going to be an awful lot to learn.

The Army's ignorance of Alaska was sensationally demonstrated in 1930 when Colonel Carl Ben Eielson crashed to his death on the coast of Siberia. Colonel Eielson, former World War flier, had done more than any other American to develop northern aviation. He had pioneered the transport of mail in Alaska and had participated several years before in an historic top-of-the-world flight from Point Barrow to Spitsbergen. When Eielson was reported missing, all available Alaskan fliers went out to search for him across the icebound Arctic, and an appeal was sent to Washington for the aid of Army planes.

No aid was forthcoming. The Army sent back word that it had no planes capable of operating in Alaska in wintertime. An appeal was then made to the Russians, and it was a group of Soviet planes that helped the Alaskans conduct the search across the icebound regions of the far north.

Much progress has been made since that day, and it is no longer accurate to say "We do not know anything about Alaska." Working at top speed to complete our new northern bases, the Army and Navy have crammed a great deal of learning and accomplishment into the space of a few years. But Alaska is still "off by itself" in the sense that it lacks an overland connection with the United States. And the job of fortifying Alaska was begun late.

This, of course, cannot be blamed on the Army and Navy alone, for it is only one of many manifestations of the general attitude of our optimistic, relatively isolated, peace-loving country—an attitude reflected in Congress and throughout the press. Yet the neglect of Alaska in the decades following World War I presents a startling contrast to the attention meted out to the island of Hawaii, which was strongly fortified in the years when Alaska, even closer to Japan, was left without means of defense.

In the 1922 Naval Armament Treaty, signed with Japan and other nations, the United States reserved the right to fortify Hawaii but agreed not to erect any defenses in the Aleutians. Although this agreement did not apply to the Alaska mainland nor to the nearer islands, nothing was done until a few years ago toward fortifying them; and even after the expiration of that armament-limiting treaty in 1936, no move was made to fortify the Aleutian chain. Not until the spring of 1939 was the first appropriation passed for Alaska's defenses: $4,000,000 for an Army cold-weather experiment station at Fairbanks. Not until the summer of 1940 was $2,900,000 appropriated for a base in the Aleutians at Dutch Harbor. Dutch Harbor is not even halfway out on the Aleutians. Beyond it the American archipelago stretches for another 850 miles toward Japan. The extent of the fortification of these more westerly islands is, of course, a military secret, but it is no secret that the work was begun still later. Despite their great strategic value, these islands were left much as they were when they were thrust up out of the ocean by the volcanic eruptions of another age. Radio stations erected on one or two of the islands were used in Pacific fleet operations, but nothing more was done and the islands remained uninhabited, except by several small villages of Aleuts, and also unvisited, except by an occasional Coast Guard cutter or Fish and Wildlife Service patrol boat and now and then by a Japanese "fishing vessel."

As late as the spring of 1940 the only armed force in Alaska was two companies of infantry stationed at Chilkoot Barracks down in the southeastern region. This post, established in the days of the Klondike gold rush, was a useless remnant of the past. The soldiers had no big guns, and even if they had, there would have been little for them to shoot there. When Governor Ernest Gruening made an official inspection trip to Chilkoot to look for quarters for the National Guard, in 1939, he found that it was no easy matter to establish contact with its sole garrison. The only available transportation was an old run-down tug, and bad weather on the Lynn Canal kept her tied up, delaying the Governor for three days. Shortly afterward, Gruening told a group of reporters that there were no Army or Navy planes in Alaska, and remarked that a few parachutists could take the Territory in short order.

Ever since his election as Alaska's Delegate eight years ago, Anthony Dimond has appealed for arms for Alaska. The tall, sparsely built, serious lawyer is the Territory's sole representative in Washington. Since Alaska has not yet acquired statehood "Tony" Dimond has no vote in Congress. Like the Delegate from Hawaii he has only the right to speak. This he does ably and eloquently, and he works harder than most voting Congressmen. Today, as Alaska gains recognition as one of America's most crucial outposts, his recommendations carry a great deal of weight. But in the past, when Tony Dimond stood up to address his colleagues, they did not always listen.

In 1935 he pointed out that Hawaii is not the only Pacific approach to the United States, and asked:

What is the use of locking one door and leaving the other one open? It is only too obvious that a hostile force moving across the Pacific could avoid Hawaii entirely and seize the coast of Alaska and as much of the mainland as required, establishing there speedily a base of attack on the northwestern and western part of the United States.

Members of Congress showed little interest in this situation, and two years later he was still at the same work.

Alaska [he warned] is today without any form of defense . . . It could be taken almost overnight by a hostile force, for there is nothing to prevent; and once in, the hostile power would have a perfect line of support from the Asian continent through the Aleutians, and the task of recapturing the Territory would be tremendous, involving millions of dollars and probably the loss of thousands of lives.

Dimond's office in the House of Representatives' building is, like Alaska, a friendly, informal place. When Alaskans come to Washington they always drop in to chat with the Delegate and his two young assistants—Mary Lee Council, daughter of the Territory's Commissioner of Health, and Wilfred Goding, who grew up in the seaport town of Skagway. The office is lined with scholarly books and cluttered with souvenirs from the Northland—an ivory bear given to Dimond by a group of Eskimos, pictures of snowcapped Mount McKinley and a pontoon plane, totem poles and fragments of mineral rock. Like most Alaskans, Tony Dimond has a strong feeling of nostalgia for the Territory all the time he is away from it. Today, this feeling is even stronger than usual. "If my people are going to get in trouble," he told me, anxiously, "I wish I could be back there with them."

It would be a mistake, however, to consider Tony Dimond a provincial. Like most other adult white Alaskans he grew up in the States. He was born, not in the far reaches of the Arctic, but on a small farm near Palatine Bridge, New York. Before he went to Alaska to prospect for gold, he farmed, taught school, worked in a locomotive factory and studied law. Like the rest of Alaska's white population—even the younger generation now growing up in the Territory—he feels American first and Alaskan second.

Aviation-conscious, like other Alaskans, Dimond knows the great strategic importance of the Territory. Facing him as he sits at his desk is a large globe. In his desk drawer he keeps a flexible ruler, and for years, over and over, he has been bending it around the North Pacific area in an attempt to show colleagues and visitors that Alaska lies on the short route between America and Asia near the top of the world.

Some people [he patiently told a Senate Committee last year] may say, "Well, let Alaska go overboard. There are only 75,000 people there, why worry about them?" Undoubtedly the attention of the Committee has been called to the fact that in the possession of the enemy Alaska will furnish a jumping-off point for invasion by air of the United States.

It is hard, these days, to get Tony Dimond to talk about anything but the war. But if you catch him in a reminiscent mood he may tell you of the time he looked for gold through the rugged mountains of the Chitina country. Prospecting for gold, he says, is the most entrancing occupation in the world. Representing Alaska in Congress all these years must have been quite the opposite. It was not till 1937, three years after his arrival in Washington, that he was able to get the matter of Alaska's fortification up for discussion on the House floor. Two years later the first appropriations were put through, but they were piddling. Even after his appeals gained increased military and naval backing they were often met with polite indifference, and sometimes even laughter. "Why would anybody want Alaska?" he was asked. In the halls of Congress, Alaska was described as a "frozen waste," much as strategic Guam was passed off by some Representatives as a "grain of sand." Some told him the Territory was so formidable a natural fortress that no one would dare to attack it. When he put his case before one high-ranking official, he was assured that there was no need to fortify Alaska because any war of the future would be fought in the Atlantic. "The Pacific," he was informed, "is going to be a great sea of peace."

There are not over two dozen men in Congress today who have been to Alaska, most of them on short trips. Few have ever known it so well as the late Senator Key Pittman who went north in the Gold Rush days and was the first city attorney at Nome. Most Senators and Representatives have never been in Alaska, and they have had, till recently, only the haziest notion of its strategic value and needs. As late as the spring of 1940, although General George Marshall, Chief of Staff, had endorsed the project, a House committee cut $68,000,000 from the Army supply bill, including $12,700,000 for an air base at Anchorage.

The House Committee, in its report refusing funds for an Alaskan air base, declared that not enough was known to determine a proper location for it. It declared that "the entire question should be canvassed and recanvassed before any commitment is made." Tony Dimond pointed out that the project had been studied and recommended by the War Department. "Delay," he warned, "would be one of those mistakes which are said to be worse than crimes."

When the matter was appealed to a Senate Committee, however, its members, too, were dubious. "Why is that base necessary?" asked one Senator. "To develop cold-weather flying?"

"What do you mean by an air base at Anchorage?" asked another.

"Is it not a fact," asked a third, "that the gulf freezes over in wintertime?"

"How far is it across there?" asked another, pointing to the straits between Alaska and Soviet Siberia. "Do you think there could be any complications in view of the distances between those two points?"

It took Hitler's invasion of Norway to restore the money for the Anchorage air base. Since then the appropriations have mounted as the war threat has increased. Today (July, 1942) they are nearing $200,000,000—over twenty-five times the amount we paid when we bought the Territory from the Russian government back in 1867.

IV

BUILDING THE BASES

THE FIRST CONTINGENT of American troops arrived in Alaska aboard the *U.S.S. St. Mihiel* in the spring of 1940. Pitching their khaki tents in a lonely field near Anchorage, swatting a few big Alaska mosquitoes, they looked about the wide, mountain-rimmed valley and asked bystanders: "Where's the air base?"

They were on it.

Today this base is the headquarters of the Alaska Defense Command.

Here, where there was nothing but wilderness, a great city of soldiers, busier and more populous than Anchorage itself, has sprung into being. Huge hangars have been built, and all day and all night, bombers and fighters roar up off the new concrete runways of nearby Elmendorf Field. Many thousands of men in uniform are living in the miles of tents and hastily constructed barracks at Fort Richardson, and for months, crowded together at night around the radios in their blacked-out quarters, they have listened tensely to short-wave reports of the war.

The Army worked at top speed to build this base. In summertime the construction never stopped. Seven days a week, in daylight and dark and in the summer all-night "dusk," rumbling bulldozers rolled up clouds of dust as they rooted out the aspen and birch to make room for barracks for the thousands of men arriving from the States. Army trucks were everywhere, stirring up more dust, which covered men, build-ings, and foliage with a gray blanket. In winter, too, the hectic building activity proceeded amidst a scene of bleak confusion. Great piles of lumber lay in the snow around the shells of new structures. Untrained soldiers marched along the slippery, hard-packed roads past dark thickets where newly installed anti-aircraft guns leaned upward toward the sky.

All over Alaska this pattern was repeated. Pilots flying their planes across the vast region looked down again and again to see busy ant-hills of military activity stirring the wilderness below. All through Alaska, barracks and hangars and gun emplacements took shape in the mud and snow on lonely sites. Speaking a few months before the Pearl Harbor attack, General Buckner told his men:

"The past year has seen our number increase from a mere handful of men in snow-covered tents to a respectable force determined to meet hostile enterprise and deal with it effec-tively. It has seen a vast construction program, the building of air bases, the fortification of these bases and the initiation of a training program calculated to weld our units into a fighting machine."

When Congress awoke to the facts of Alaska's location three years ago, the building of these northern bases was begun in haste; and all through 1941 Alaska was full of work and hectic confusion and urgency. Not until months after the Pearl Harbor attack did the States begin to rival this dis-play of war. As fast as boats could be loaded, they steamed to Alaska jammed to bursting with defense workers and sup-plies. Over twenty thousand construction workers migrated north in two years. Soldiers swarmed up faster than barracks could be built to house them. The towns near the bases were thronged with officers and privates from all over the States.

Trucks and jeeps tore up and down the streets. The crowded bars and restaurants looked like canteens. It seemed as if Alaska were one great army camp, with most of its population in uniform.

No details, of course, may be published regarding the stage of completion of the Alaskan bases, or of the number of men and planes stationed there. The situation, furthermore, is changing so fast that any statements made today will be obsolete tomorrow. However, as of July, 1942, two general observations may be made. On the one hand, it is a published fact that appropriations for the Alaskan defenses still total less than half of what was spent on the fortifying of Hawaii. From this, any citizen can readily realize that Alaska is hardly a "giant fortress," as some writers have called it. On the other hand, the development of the Alaskan bases was, according to a Navy statement, "far ahead of progress originally hoped for in their construction," and the Army, too, has outstripped its original schedules, accomplishing much more than had been hoped for, in the short time since the work was initiated.

The construction of the Alaskan bases has been an extraordinary job. In these days of all-out war activity, when bomber factories are taking shape almost overnight on the sites of apple orchards, the Alaskan fortification may seem like a routine achievement. It was much more than that. It was a frontier task, in a strange and little-known region of treacherous, fog-bound coasts, huge unexplored mountains, and permanently frozen inland plains—a no-man's-land with almost no population, offering almost no developed means of food or fuel supply. A country of vast distances, and a country that lacked any form of overland connection with the States.

If the Congressmen who appropriated the funds for Alaska's fortification knew very little about the Territory, the

Army, when it started north, did not know a great deal more. The Navy, too, had a lot to learn—especially about the Aleutians. They had to find out the hard way, grappling with bewildering new problems as they went along. In a sense, these men have "discovered" Alaska more extensively than it was ever discovered before. They were all explorers: the officers and the ordinary buck privates, and also the construction workers—welders, powder monkeys, structural iron workers and carpenters like those with whom I traveled to Alaska aboard the *Mt. McKinley*. Long before they docked at Dutch Harbor, these men began to realize why it was a tough proposition to prepare Alaska for war.

Two days after we left Seattle the *Mt. McKinley* moved through Dixon Entrance past the Canadian boundary, and a procession of white peaks became visible off to the East.

"We're in Alaska now," the purser told us; but the country ahead looked the same as it had before. As the boat continued to churn through the steep fjords, there was still no sign of civilization. The spruce trees on shore were getting lower and more stunted as on the ascent of a mountain. The gulls following the ship had white instead of black-tipped wings, another sign of the North. Although we had not been traveling long, some of us got the feeling that we were approaching the top of the globe.

"When do we get to a city?" one man asked the purser.

Several were beginning to feel restive, wondering how soon they would get out of the wilderness. But they discovered in the days that followed that they were not going to get out of the wilderness, so long as they stayed in Alaska.

There is nothing about Alaska that impresses visitors so much as its size. Getting to the Alaskan boundary is easy as compared to moving from one part of Alaska to another.

Alaska is one-fifth as large as the States, and with the far-flung Aleutian chain stretching almost all the way to Asia, the Territory's shape makes it seem even larger than it actually is. From east to west, Alaska is as far across as from New York to California, and in traveling the length of the territory including the Aleutians you have to turn your watch back five hours, two more than when you cross the States.

Back in 1703 a sailor who had been shipwrecked in Alaska came home to report that he saw men "as tall as an ordinary spire-steeple, taking ten yards at a stride, speaking many degrees louder than a speaking trumpet in voices so high in the air that it sounded like thunder." In over two hundred years the country has hardly been touched, and modern travelers are so affected by its lonely distances and heights that they, too, are apt to tell tall stories. It is a land that should be peopled by giants. Yet, for the most part, it is not even peopled by men. In all the vast region there are very few towns; and most of those, scattered along its southern shore, are so tiny and so isolated that they only accentuate the sense of wilderness.

Although we had been looking for it for hours, we were startled when our steamer pulled into sight of Ketchikan, first port of call in Alaska. The ship was gliding along the mirror-still water winding through the lonely forests, when suddenly she rounded a bend and there in front of us was a typical American main street, crowded with jostling people and parked automobiles. It ran down to the water's edge, with a big sign "WELCOME VISITORS" hung across the middle of it. The workers crowded down the gangplank. Some of them found their way into the Blue Fox bar, where juke boxes were playing the same tunes they had been playing back home. Others drifted into the Stedman, ordered Broadway

Building the Bases 43

Kelly sundaes and played a game of pool in the room next door. Wandering along the wooden-fronted curving streets, they passed the O. K. Barber Shop, the New Deal Cocktail Bar, the A. & P., the Elks Headquarters, the A.F. of L. Union Hall. It looked like any town in the Western States; and yet, at the same time, there was something quite different about it.

The difference was that there was nothing there but Ketchikan. Behind it the mountains rose sheer and steep, with clouds of fog drifting above timberline. There were no highways leading out of Ketchikan past tourist camps and filling stations, no sign-posts pointing to cities beyond. Out of Ketchikan, a car could not bump very far over the rough road before it would come to a dead-end stop in deep, unbroken forest. There was an appealing bravado about the bustling little town with all its automobiles, for it really clung by itself onto the edge of nowhere. Behind it lay nothing but vast wilderness; before it stretched even vaster spaces of sea.

When the *Mt. McKinley* blew her whistle in a half-hour warning, the workers wandered back and climbed aboard. As she pulled away from the dock a few stragglers came running down the street, and she had to turn back to pick them up. When she moved off again, a slow, drizzling rain began to fall; and, looking back, we saw that the fog, rolling down from the mountains, had enveloped much of the town. Only a few half-houses were visible, with scattered bright neon lights flashing through the murky gloom. Soon the *Mt. McKinley* was pursuing her lonely course again through the fjords, and it seemed as if the houses and docks of Ketchikan had been a mirage.

The episode was repeated over and over. Much of Alaska's population lives in steep-streeted towns that cling to mountainsides at the edge of the sea, lonely port towns that are cut off from all land communication. As one of the construction workers remarked: "These joints are O. K., but it's a hell of a long way between them."

As the steamer moved out of Icy Straits into the Gulf of Alaska the workers looked ahead to a sea of tossing whitecaps. Now they were entering an even lonelier part of the Territory where there were no signs of civilization at all. Waves smacked against the ship's bow and the water splashed across her deck as a gale began to blow. To the east the huge Fairweather Range appeared, mighty snowcaps rising up to fifteen thousand feet sheer from the sea. Clouds of fog hung along the peaks and over the glaciers that spewed crashing bergs into the ocean. The sight was so magnificent that it was almost frightening. In most parts of the world such a panorama can be seen only by daring explorers after fatiguing climbs through rough and difficult terrain; but in Alaska it passes before the eyes of ordinary travelers as they lounge on the deck of a ship.

"God," said a steamfitter, "how are you going to defend a thing like that?"

"How would anybody invade it?" asked another, taking a swig from the ever present bottle.

The men still had a long, long way to go. Rocking across the rough waters of the Gulf, the boat swung off "to the Westward" in the direction of Japan. As it passed along the Alaska Peninsula, the rugged precipitous mountain peaks began to taper down into the sea, to become the pinnacled rocky islands of the Aleutian chain. The thick forests had tapered, too, so that now the land was covered only with a scraggly growth of small stunted trees and gnarled bushes. Here and there a snowcapped peak stood high out of the water, smoking with volcanic fires. Beyond False Pass there were no trees of any kind—the only trees on the Aleutian chain are a small clump of ancient spruce planted by the Russians at Unalaska. There were no signs of life, except screaming gulls and great colonies of black and white murres clustering along the rocky ledges. It was a desolate spectacle, and the men were glad when the ship finally docked at the foot of Ballyhoo Mountain in the midst of the busy war activity of Dutch Harbor.

Till recently, Dutch Harbor was the westernmost base on Alaska's far-flung island chain, with the Navy's other air and submarine bases spaced like stepping-stones between it and Seattle; the major ones located at Sitka (near the southeastern Panhandle) and Kodiak (off the base of the Alaska Peninsula). After the war began, work was speeded "off the record" at other points along the Aleutian chain.

The Army's job is on the mainland. The Anchorage air base, near the middle of Alaska's wide southern span, commands both the coast and the Interior, and is located on the tracks of the Alaska Railroad. At inland Fairbanks, northern terminus of the railroad, another major air base has been built, and military airports built by the Civil Aeronautics Administration are being rushed to completion at widely scattered points throughout the region. Both Army and Navy, however, have concentrated their Alaskan bases along the southern coast and the Aleutians.

Alaska's wartime operations are closely tied to those of the West Coast States. Currently, General Buckner reports to Fourth Army Headquarters at San Francisco; the head of the Navy in Alaska, on the other hand, reports to the Thirteenth Naval District in Seattle. To date (July, 1942) no one officer has been placed in charge of the entire Alaska operation. General Buckner as head of the Army's Defense Command is the nearest thing to it. His troops are stationed at both the Navy and the Army bases, and he has been the ranking officer in the Territory during its transformation from a defenseless wilderness into a fortified outpost.

When Congress passed the first appropriation for Alaskan bases, the Army realized that it was confronted with an enormously complex task. So little was known about Alaska, and its problems were so different from any the Army had ever faced, that routine methods could not apply. The man in charge of the Alaska Defense Command would have to be a builder who could improvise as he went along. It was a job for a soldier with imagination and General Buckner was the answer.

The General, a strapping, ruddy-complexioned, white-haired Kentuckian, is one of the Army's leading schoolmasters, distinguished for his knowledge of strategy and tactics. He has taught at both Fort Leavenworth and the Army War College, and was executive officer of the latter for several years. More recently he spent four years as Commandant of the Cadet Corps at West Point. At the time of his appointment to Alaska he was Chief of Staff of the Sixth Division.

When I interviewed General Buckner at Fort Richardson I was surprised by the jovial manner of this tough and scholarly soldier. As he leaned back from his desk, discussing Alaska's strategic situation, two black and white setters dozed peacefully on the floor beside him. There was little in the atmosphere to suggest the imminent death and destruction in the Pacific. Alaska, he told me, is much nearer than Hawaii to Japan. Alaska has great offense possibilities. As he expounded these facts in an affable Southern accent, one of the dogs scrambled to her feet from time to time and roamed uneasily about the office until a snap of the General's fingers brought her back to the floor.

Buckner is an enthusiastic sportsman and brought his setters all the way north with him from Kentucky. He likes to get up before dawn in winter blizzards, take a boat, and go out looking for ducks, or, hopping a plane, to fly off and fish in Alaska's famous trout streams in the Kenai and Bristol Bay regions.

"In the States," the General once told a friend, "men like to lie about their fishing. In Alaska a man can't lie about fishing because the truth is unbelievable, so he has to lie about something else."

In the months before war began the General was engaged in a bitter controversy with the Alaska Game Commission, because it required Army men stationed in Alaska to pay the same high hunting-license fees as non-resident sportsmen from the States. When Commission officials refused the General resident status, he took the issue to court.

General Buckner likes Alaska's magnificent rough country so much that he has had plans drawn for a house near Anchorage with a view of snowcapped Mt. McKinley, and hopes to settle down there upon retirement. None of the Territory's primitive conditions has fazed the General; he has, in fact, enjoyed his northern assignment, because it has involved doing a job "from the ground up."

In outlining the problems of the Alaskan operation General Buckner stressed one thing above all others: the difficulty of transportation and supply.

There was no overland connection over which supplies could be moved to the heart of Alaska. While a Canadian railroad extended west to Prince Rupert just south of the Alaska Panhandle region, a provision of the Jones Act, inserted at the behest of railroad and steamship interests, forbade its use for Alaska-bound freight. Not until the war began was this provision revoked. Even then, the route was of little significance as a means of supply to Alaska's major Army bases, and during most of the construction period the Army has had to move all its heavy supplies north from Seattle by boat.

This was especially important because of the dearth of supplies available within the near-wilderness region. The Army and Navy had to ship north almost all the cement and lumber and steel to build the bases, and all the ammunition, gas, and oil to supply them. They had to take up most of the skilled workers to the job. For all these many thousands of workers, as well as for the troops, they had to provide housing on the lonely sites and they also had to provide food. In other words, they had to import a whole, self-contained economy, hauling it north to Alaska on small crowded boats.

As the construction workers on the *Mt. McKinley* saw, it is no simple matter to navigate a ship through the narrow, fogbound channels of the inside Alaska route which is usually followed. In addition, Alaska's unusually high tides cause frequent trouble in loading and unloading at the docks. When the Army tried to take some of its transports into Anchorage, it had to buck the fast, powerful, thirty-foot tides of Cook Inlet. The harbor there is full of floating ice in winter, and no large commercial ship had tried to enter it for years.

But it was when they swung westward toward the unknown Aleutians that the ships really encountered trouble. To call the navigation of the Aleutians a pioneer job is something of an understatement. As recently as 1941 an article in the *U. S. Naval Institute Proceedings* stated: "At this time no charts exist of the great majority of the Aleutian indentations, and many of those that do exist cannot be trusted."

Yet the shores of these islands are a maze of complicated bays, channels and inlets, full of rocks and pinnacles and exceedingly difficult to navigate even under the best conditions. As described by a Navy officer in the *Proceedings*:

Many of these dangerous pinnacles have been found through disastrous shipwrecks. The straits between the islands vary in width from yards to several miles. They are deep, but are dotted with occasional pinnacles and other unmarked dangers. Currents in the straits are often swift and erratic. While there are differences in the islands, it is extremely difficult to tell them apart even after long experience. When to this is added the ever present fog, concealing the coast and foothills of one island and the tops and peaks of the next, it is apparent that navigation about the islands is not an unmixed pleasure.

Since war began the Coast Guard has installed many new signals along the rugged, winding, indented Alaskan coast, and Navy ships are patrolling its length. Out along the Aleutians, the Navy has commandeered the help of local fishermen whose halibut boats and cannery tenders are known as "Y.P." (Yard Patrol) boats. The Commander of the Aleutian patrol, a Seldovia cannery man, C. E. ("Squeaky") Anderson, sports a weather-beaten plaid shirt along with his official Navy cap, and zestfully uses his own personal "know-how" to navigate the strategic waters. But few skippers know these waters like Squeaky Anderson; and so the commercial ships and transports, steaming westward with supplies for the Aleutian bases, face constant hazards.

Shipping supplies to the southern and Aleutian bases was only part of the transportation difficulty faced in fortifying Alaska. Not only is Alaska as broad as the whole continental United States. From north to south it is also nearly as deep.

The Army found that it had to cope with not one country

but three. Back of the steep, mountainous area of the southern coast, the mainland lies hundreds of miles north and west in one huge rolling plain, covered with patches of forest, great curling rivers, and a multitude of lakes. Up north of the Arctic Circle another jagged mountain range rises out of the tundra, and beyond these unexplored peaks the land flattens out again into wide, sandy beaches fronting on the Arctic Ocean.

Since the waters north and northwest of Alaska are ice-bound in winter down to the Pribilof Islands, there are only a few months in the year when it is possible to ship heavy supplies to those coasts. But it was the deep inland region that represented the real transportation problem. As one officer remarked: "There are very few ports where you can land things and get them anywhere." The government-owned Alaska Railroad, running up from the port town of Seward to Fairbanks, is the only railroad of any length in the whole Territory. There is also only one road of any length—the 371-mile Richardson Highway (also built by the federal government), starting at Valdez and running inland in the same general direction as the railroad. It is of low-grade surface and has always been snow-blocked for several months during the winter. Like the railroad, it terminates at Fairbanks with an extension, the Steese Highway, reaching 162 miles further inland.

Fairbanks, the "Golden Heart of the Interior," lies on the bend of a river in the middle of the Tanana Valley. It is the only town of any size in all inland Alaska. To reach it, you must cross the lonely tundra for hours, and as your plane approaches it, Fairbanks looks almost as lost in the vast rolling valley as the steep port towns look along the edge of the sea.

Until the war program was undertaken, it was not possible to drive a car between Anchorage and Fairbanks; the railroad was the only connection between them. Soon after the Army arrived, the government began construction of a cross-country link to connect the Anchorage road system with the Richardson Highway. The Army also began work on a new tunnel and harbor project on Prince William Sound which will provide the Interior with a more accessible ice-free port, eliminating the tunneled, tortuous railroad journey up through the mountains from Seward to Anchorage.

Except for this small strip of civilization along the railroad belt, the Army found that inland Alaska was for the most part untracked and unpopulated, and that less than half of it had been mapped. The difficulty of getting around in the vast inland and northern regions of Alaska is illustrated by the slowness of the Territory's first draft. The Selective Service Administration had to borrow Army bombers and parachute the necessary papers and forms down to remote Eskimo villages like Kanakanak, Kotzebue, Bethel, and Barrow. The Director did not receive until August a letter from one of his outlying boards that had been mailed in May, and he spent a month and a half making the rounds of the local boards by plane.

The Army, too, used planes wherever it could. The most complicated transportation problem encountered in fortifying Alaska was that of moving heavy, unflyable equipment. It was faced not so much by the Army as by the Civil Aeronautics Administration, which had the job of building most of the inland airports and air fields. The only way it could move heavy machinery and supplies to remote inland points was to take them up the rivers by boat during the summer, then wait until the first winter snow when they could be hauled across country by "cat" train.

Alaskan supply coordination was rendered unusually difficult by the ever recurring transportation obstacle. Work was sometimes held up for weeks, even months, for small items, such as pumps and special pipe fittings. In the States these can usually be trucked to a job without delay; but in Alaska, according to an official Army statement issued for release on December 7, 1941, "if special equipment or a spare part is suddenly needed, it is necessary to radio the District Office. This office makes the procurement and then ships it by vessel. Shipment sometimes requires ten days if the ship happens to be sailing at about the time the material is ready, and also if the ship is going directly to that location. Such a combination of favorable connections seldom occurs. Usually much more time is required from the initial request until the material reaches its destination in Alaska." It is small wonder that occasional embarrassing boners were pulled, such as the arrival of iceboxes at the Air Corps cold-weather experiment station before the barracks were built, and of electric stoves at Seward although the local power plant had no extra juice available to supply them.

When the transportation job was finished, another obstacle was faced—that of difficult terrain. Down on the rain-drenched southern coast the land was covered with muskeg—a spongy vegetable growth sometimes running fifteen feet deep, and often filled with embedded branches and logs. All this had to be torn up, and a rock fill laid, before the Army could begin work. At Yakutat it rained constantly, so that at times the newly mixed concrete was ruined before it had a chance to set. This was solved by covering the runways with a huge, rolling marquee which they towed along on a tractor to cover the cement as it dried and hardened.

In the more northerly inland regions, the difficulties were of another kind. There the tundra-covering acts as an insulator, and the subsoil remains permanently frozen. Wherever possible this ground was avoided, and the air fields were put on gold-dredge tailings or on the silt left by wandering rivers. In one case, they could not avoid it, and had to construct a heated tunnel to protect the water, sewage, and power system; and in the winter months workers sometimes had to thaw their coal and many of their construction materials. The long hours of Arctic darkness also constituted a problem— yet it is in winter that military operations would be most successfully performed in these northern regions. Fighting in Alaska would be similar to fighting in Finland; in the hot summers the tundra turns into a soupy swamp, nearly impassable to machines of war; but in winter, tractors and tanks can operate across the snow-covered plains, and the lakes are frozen hard.

In the months before war began, as everyone in Alaska knew, one of the Army's biggest anxieties was the low morale of the troops. This was especially true at the dreary island bases where it rained or stormed incessantly. The soldiers watched high-paid construction workers coming and going. Many of these workers did not stick for long—but the soldiers had to stay. A large portion were draftees, many of them from Southern States like Alabama, Florida and Texas, and were spending their first winter in tents.

Some of the soldiers, to be sure, found things they liked about Alaska. At the cold weather bases the men got fancy muskrat and reindeer parkas, mukluks, dark goggles. Some learned to ski. (Two soldiers, born in Arkansas, who had never seen snow before their induction into the Army, recently won first and second honors in the annual cross-country ski races at Nome.) Some liked Alaska so much they planned to stay after the war. The Kodiak *Bear*, published by the soldiers at the Fort Greely Naval Air Station, declared: "Many of us will come back as civilians. . . . We'll bring our wives and our youngsters. We'll bring plows and carpenters' tools. We'll plant seeds in the rich earth. . . ." In another issue, the *Bear* congratulated a soldier for being in Alaska four months and "not even trying to write a poem about it."

The giant, rugged, forbidding country never fails to make a powerful impression on newcomers. Some soldiers bought cameras to take shots of the magnificent scenery—as everyone wants to who goes to Alaska. And some did try to write poems. But many others were more in a mood for profanity.

Mails were slow and uncertain. There were almost no recreation facilities. The men had little to do in their spare time, and crowded into the bars and saloons. On pay day they drank scotch and rye—the rest of the time they sipped their beer slowly and watched the high-paid construction workers downing hard liquor. The scarcity of women was the chief complaint. "It wouldn't be so bad," one soldier told me, "if a guy had a dame up here. What the hell! It wouldn't cost much. There's nice scenery—the mountains, and glaciers, and all that. But, boy, I'll take my scenery on a postcard any day in the week. This place is dead. It ain't got nothing."

The Alaska blues took many forms, but it always got down to the same question. "What are we here for?" the men asked. "We'll never see action."

But the Pearl Harbor attack changed the atmosphere. From that time on, all minds were turned to the Westward.

"Merry Christmas, Men!" said a Kodiak *Bear* headline. "Lights Are Dim but Hearts Are Light." Advising townsfolk to dig themselves air-raid shelters, the *Bear* declared: "We'll always drink Beer, not Saki." The sheet was full of humorous pluck, lively with restlessness for action.

Many of the men, according to the *Bear,* were ordering globes with which to follow the progress of the war. One private fell out of bed, dreaming that he was fighting the Japs. Another got a V-for-Victory haircut. "Two More Bombing Days Till Christmas," the *Bear* announced. "If the Japs Bomb Us, Let's Embalm Them." And the men began wishing each other a "Jappy New Year!"

Ever since the war started, the soldiers in Alaska have been impatient for an offensive. A "Kayo to Tokyo" club, started at Fort Richardson, has spread fast, its members agreeing to pay off for every enemy plane downed by Allied fliers. A young officer at Fort Richardson, writing in the spring of 1942, declared:

It is becoming completely apparent that the only way to beat the Japs is to go over and personally accomplish the task. Our minds are being drawn constantly to the Westward. . . . This state of "straining at the leash" is absorbing every man in Alaska. . . .

I have personally heard many officers and men state that the great chain of the Aleutian Islands should be our springboard, and like impatient swimmers on a warm spring day they are anxious to try that springboard . . . and dive right into Tokyo.

As bombers and pursuit ships take off on routine patrols, the hearts of the men on the ground go with them. Not every one is lucky enough to go soaring across the lonely wilderness of Alaska to meet that possible aerial combat, but somehow the mobility of the planes creates a restlessness within us to get going along that springboard.

Tokyo gets closer every day in our minds. . . . Gradually the great strategic importance of Alaska and the fighting men stationed there is being realized, and being realized where it counts the most . . . in the minds of the soldiers of the Alaska Defense Command.

V

FLYING THE PLANES

As WAR WORKERS struggled with forbidding terrain—stripping off the muskeg, felling the forests, blasting off the tops of rocky islands, they had one primary objective—to build facilities for planes. What they were constructing was a far-flung chain of mainland and island air bases from which several thousand bombers and fighters could operate. In planning the strategy of Alaska, both Army and Navy have placed their main emphasis on aviation.

This was not surprising to the Alaskans. They are the most air-minded people under the American flag. Although Alaska is in general an undeveloped region, in this one respect it is extraordinarily progressive. Thousands of Alaskan children living in remote mining and trading settlements like Chicken and Fishhook and Grubstake and Coffee Creek and Savage River and Lucky Shot—children who have never seen a train or an automobile—take the airplane as a matter of course. "Everybody flies" in Alaska—senators, miners, fishermen, salesmen, trappers—whites and Indians and Eskimos, all crowded together in the high-winged monoplanes that soar hour after hour above the wilderness between towns. For long-distance travel the dog team is fast becoming obsolete. Across the vast regions of the Interior "everything flies," too: food, oil, radio batteries, schoolbooks, hospital supplies, even mining machinery, all are carried by air.

For years the Alaskans have watched planes hovering above

the mountains and tundra and coming in for landings, little ships on pontoons sliding down onto the water of the lakes and fjords, little ships on skis making neat parallel tracks as they land on the deep snow, little ships on wheels bumping down onto river bars and rough clearings. But today they are seeing strange new planes roaring down, fast, onto long military runways—enormous, green-brown camouflaged ships of war with many metal propellers and long glassed-in noses, big ships the like of which most of them had never seen before.

As there is no hum of traffic or industry in Alaska's small frontier towns, everybody hears a plane as it circles for a landing or as it soars in a take-off. The sputtering motor of a small Gullwing Stinson, echoing and reechoing from the mountains that rise steeply behind the coastal towns, seems to make much more racket than a transcontinental over New York. Today the thunder of bombers and pursuits seems almost deafening, and the Alaskans, looking skyward through the windows of their homes, wonder, as few other Americans wonder, "Are they ours?"

"U.S. Planes Fly Over Yukon," an *Alaska Weekly* headline announced shortly after the Hawaii attack. "Big Bombers Head North from Outside Fields to Reinforce Alaska Defense Projects." The story gives a vivid glimpse of the way in which war first became real to the people of the northland.

Going into Whitehorse airport after dark one evening, following his local flight from Dawson south via Mayo and the local route, Pilot Les Cook had a rare experience. Just as Les was landing the Kingbird, a huge bird of the air zoomed over him. The Yukon ace didn't have to think twice to know that it was no usual plane zooming above his ship. In fact, he thought to himself, "It's the Japs for sure."

But it wasn't!

As it happened, it was one of Uncle Sam's big, speedy, stream-

lined bombers just coming in from Edmonton. Five such ships—
B-26 bombers, the class of the U.S.A. bombing fleet—landed in
Whitehorse airport that night.

Their destination—ask someone who knows. This is war—and
army planes don't talk. At any rate, wherever they were headed,
you can be mighty sure they were well prepared to give the enemy
the works.

No one wished he were up there in the front office of the huge
war plane any more than pilot Cook.

The Army and Navy have placed their main emphasis on
aviation, but at the time their program was begun Alaska was
next to useless for aerial warfare. The region, one of the
greatest potential offense bases in the world, did not have a
single air field on which a large bomber could be landed with
safety. The federal government had spent virtually nothing to
develop northern aviation.

To be sure, there were over a hundred fields scattered
throughout the region. Federal road-building equipment was
used for some, and funds provided, but most were financed by
Alaska itself. Miners working new creeks in the Interior region
cut and cleared many of these small fields out of the scraggly
timber and frozen swamp as soon as they set up camp. These
clearings are adequate for the small craft used by the Alaskans, but their runways are much too short for the planes of
war. According to one popular story, an Alaskan pilot flying
his small plane Outside in the States, after swooping down
for an emergency landing on a narrow river bar, turned and
laughed at the terror on his passengers' faces. "What's the
matter?" he asked. "Why, in Alaska this would be an airport."

When Pan American pioneered its service into Alaska from
Seattle, it had to build its own field at the capital town of
Juneau. At Anchorage the old municipal field got so muddy
in the spring breakup that there were weeks when it could **not**

be used. The people of Fairbanks well remember that when Howard Hughes took off from their field in 1938 on his round-the-world flight, his heavily loaded plane almost brushed the tops of the trees. These fields were the best in the Territory.

Down in the steep, precipitous coastal Panhandle region there were few places level enough to lay a runway. Towns like Ketchikan, Petersburg, and Wrangell had no fields. A few years ago, when a lost ship "on wheels" appeared over Ketchikan, the local pilot Ray Renshaw, who went up to help, could think of no way out but to lead it to a shallow seaside cove. There the plane dropped to a rough crash landing in the mud, and its passengers thanked their stars it happened to be low tide. Alaskans flying in this region use pontoon ships which can "set down" on the protected waters of the fjords, or on the nearby inland lakes. Most Alaskan coastal flying is of this "puddle-jumping" variety.

In wintertime when planes can land anywhere in the snow, much of the flying in the inland regions is done on skis, and the frozen lakes provide excellent landing places for wheeled planes—even the heavy planes of war. Up along the northwest and Arctic coasts there are wide stretches of hard-packed sandy beach on which large war planes can make emergency landings on wheels. But these natural landing fields were of limited value, being remote from points of supply.

Alaska not only was without adequate fields at the time the military program began; but it also was without radio ranges, beacons, and other modern aviation aids; and until recently all flying was "contact." Although the Alaskans had established their own informal system of weather reporting, it was, according to the Civil Aeronautics Administration, "disorganized and inadequate," and most of the weather reports were hours old. Alaskan pilots have a reputation for being among the best in the world—"because they have to be." As the Anchorage *Times* described it a few years ago: "Flying in Alaska depended entirely on the skill and experience of the pilot, for once he left his port no more was heard of him until he landed at his destination, or came hiking into a roadhouse after sitting down on a river bar or some frozen lake." Alaskan fliers always carry guns and food supplies for use if they are forced down in the wilderness.

Although Pan American's larger planes, equipped with transocean-type long-range direction finders, could fly "over the top," even these flew "contact" much of the time, hovering close to the ground and watching the terrain below them —below them, or sometimes *around* them, as on the trip I made from Juneau to Fairbanks in an Electra. Flying along one of the steep and rugged passes of the coastal mountain range, great rocky peaks surrounding us on both sides, we soon began to pass shifting patches of white mist blowing along the slopes. They rapidly got thicker and, as we looked ahead, it seemed as if we were about to plunge into a sea of dense fog. "Don't see how he can get through that," muttered the fat, goggled contractor who occupied the seat across from me, fiddling with his safety belt and stretching to look out the window. Just at this point the plane banked sharply and turned back to try another route.

Turning back has long been an established custom of Alaskan aviation, with the skillful pilots continuing their routes only so far as they could see their course. In the northern regions the summer season of the midnight sun makes it possible to fly all the time; but the winters are long and dark and, throughout the Territory, operations were seldom carried on except in daylight. When the military program began, only two fields in all Alaska were equipped with night beacons.

The Army pilots had constant difficulty trying to operate

under these primitive conditions. It is no simple job for a plane to find its way across the confusing pattern of tundra, lakes, and rivers of the inland regions. And to make things worse, the compass behaves erratically in many parts of Alaska because of the country's extensive mineralization. Even local fliers have had trouble finding their way in "contact" flights over the Interior. According to Joe Crosson, pioneer of Alaska aviation and now manager of Pan American's Alaska Division, "It's hard to tell which way the rivers are running, and it's sometimes tough to 'pick up' a town." When Joe Crosson says this, it means a great deal, for he has had long years of experience in Alaskan aviation, and other fliers will tell you that he has a kind of sixth sense about finding his way in the northland wilderness.

Crosson has accomplished many mercy flights, helped many lost pilots. When the late Wiley Post crossed from Russia into Alaska on his round-the-world solo flight, he lost his way and made a forced landing at Flat, cracking his propeller. When Joe Crosson, 360 miles away at Fairbanks, heard the news, he immediately loaded a spare propeller into his own plane and flew to Flat, repaired the damaged ship, helped Post aboard, and led him on to Fairbanks. This was an easy trip, but some of Crosson's flights have been extremely hazardous. In the summer of 1937, as soon as he heard that the Russian North Pole fliers were lost, he got busy organizing a three-way search expedition. He himself took the hardest job, heading north in his Electra over the wild tundra, circling out over the Arctic Ocean, and returning over the perpetual snow and the live glaciers of the jagged Brooks mountains. He scanned some 80,000 square miles before landing in Fairbanks. Another plane flew north and east to Fort Yukon, covering the "badlands" of the Skeenjack and Christian rivers, returning by way of Beaver; and the third plane, on floats, circled the Wild Lake country. The Russians were not sighted, but in five hours Joe Crosson and his men scanned a large part of northern Alaska.

Joe Crosson is the most famous living Alaskan pilot, and his name is well known in the States. Inside the Territory itself, however, there are other fliers who are fully as famous, and who are at least his equal in skill and daring. There is Jack Jefford, senior patrol pilot of the Civil Aeronautics Administration, who has flown the Territory for seven years. The Eskimos and Indians call him "Owl Eyes" because of his miraculous ability to find his way over the Arctic regions, even in the dark. When Jack Jefford comes into a Yukon or Kuskokwim village, the natives hustle around his plane and put themselves out for him in every possible way. He, too, is beloved for his mercy flights. There is Shell Simmons who has flown the winding coastline for a great many years. He is one of the most uncanny float pilots in Alaska. As his ship hovers across the labyrinth of islets and steep mountains, he is exceptionally adept at judging wind velocities and fog speeds and distances. He, too, is known for his courage: his scarred face still bears the marks of a crash he had some years ago when, badly injured and with his nose torn to shreds, he dove into the water and rescued every one of his passengers. Then, leaving them as comfortable as possible, he walked several miles to the nearest settlement to summon help. These are only a few of the heroic, matter-of-fact men who, without fanfare, have developed American flying in the Far North.

Today, federal funds are pouring into Alaska for new aviation facilities, with results far more revolutionary than is generally realized. The mainland fields that are being constructed by the Civil Aeronautics Administration to supplement the

Army and Navy bases are vital to the scheme of war—and will have great permanent value in time of peace. A brand-new modern airway is being established. Already, the Army and Navy and large scheduled airlines are flying their Alaska routes "over the top" on instruments, and conditions are rapidly being brought to a par with those of the States.

Although the Civil Aeronautics Administration began its Alaskan airways program in 1939, it was not until early in 1941 that it received funds for the construction of military airports. It has worked fast with its mounting appropriations, and workers are leveling the ground and pouring the cement for a network of over thirty airports and intermediate fields. They are building them at widely scattered points throughout the region from Northway, where a twenty-foot swath cut out of the timber marks the Alaska-Canada boundary, to Nome, just across the strait from Siberia, and at points deep in the Interior.

The building of these fields has been a hasty and spectacular job, and Marshall Hoppin, manager of the Civil Aeronautics Administration in Alaska, deserves much credit for the speed with which it has been performed. Hoppin, a tall, efficient man, started his career in dirt-track racing; but he decided, after his first airplane ride, that automobiles were not fast enough. He served as an instructor and pilot in World War I, and has been in aviation ever since. For a while he owned three planes and ran a charter service in Illinois, Ohio, and Indiana, and he barnstormed all over the country until he went with the CAA in 1927. He worked for them twelve years (most of that time in airport development) before they sent him up to Alaska.

When Mr. Hoppin got his funds for military airports in January, 1941, he put his men to work at a feverish rate of speed, selecting the sites and collecting the preliminary engineering data so that construction could begin that summer. "Those fields had to be ready yesterday," says Mr. Hoppin. Although some of them had to be hacked out of the frozen tundra and forest, hundreds of miles from the nearest sizable town—all were usable by the end of that year. Even before the runways were paved, the planes bumped down onto the rough, earthen surfaces, and lanterns or blazing barrels of oil guided the Army fliers through the night. Aviation aids were installed as fast as possible, and today newly trained pilots from the States, flying hour after hour across strange country in the dark, are relieved to pick up the beams of these modern northland fields, to see the flash of their beacons in the midst of forbidding wilderness. New weather stations, too, are being installed all over the Territory from points far out on the Aleutians up to the distant reaches of the Arctic Coast, and when the current program is complete, Alaska will have at least two hundred of them: some with radiosonde and pilot balloon equipment, many reporting hourly, all reporting several times a day.

No aspect of Alaska's military program is more important than this one; bad weather has been a constant problem to the Army and Navy, presenting a far subtler and more treacherous obstacle than any difficulty of terrain. The forces of nature seem to have played an ironic trick when they formed Alaska: its unique ocean-bridging location makes it one of the most strategic air bases anywhere. It was a great gift, but it seems to have been given grudgingly—for Alaska has some of the worst flying weather in the whole world.

This is true, it must be emphasized, only in one part of Alaska—the precipitous southern coast and island chain, where the climate is moist and "oceanic." It is not true of the arid inland region behind the coastal mountain ranges, where flying conditions are excellent. On December 7, when the coast was swept with fog and sleet storms, it was a clear, bright day at Fairbanks. This contrast is typical, and it may prove decisive to the course of battle in Alaska.

Many Americans think that cold is the big problem in Alaska, but this is not the case. Bitter, sub-zero weather, which exists only in the inland and northern regions, is far less of a problem than some of the conditions along the warm southern coast. Cold weather presents no obstacle to aviation once the tricks of the trade have been learned.

The first Army project begun in Alaska under the defense program was Ladd Field, Air Corps Cold Weather Experiment Station at Fairbanks. Fairbanks is south of the Arctic Circle, and it may seem strange that a point farther north was not chosen for cold-weather experimental work. The fact is that coastal climates are always tempered by the sea, and it does not get so cold along the northern coast as it does in the more arid Interior. Even in this Interior region Alaska does not get much colder than the States; its record winter temperature of 76° below zero is only ten degrees lower than the record in the States (66° below at the Riverside Ranger Station, Wyoming). The difference is that in Alaska it stays colder longer.

Long before the Army began its cold-weather experimenting, Pan American and sourdough pilots had worked out many of the problems of operating in the winter North. Ten years ago Pan American began carrying the winter Star Route mail from Fairbanks to Nome, with dozens of stops at the small settlements along the way. The route was pioneered on skis, the planes landing in the snow on runways marked off with flares or small spruce trees. The company found out how to get along without heated hangars, keeping "nightgowns" on the wings and warming the motors with "plumber's stoves"; how to take care of fuel at temperatures so low that a strip of oil poured into the snow can be handled "like a stick of wood"; how to clothe its pilots to protect them from freezing, in the case of forced landings; how to tie a plane onto a frozen lake with an "ice bridge" to keep it from blowing away in a gale. Much of the local experience was useful to the Army. Many Alaskan pilots feel that the Army could utilize this experience far more extensively than it has to date. This may be true, but in any case the Army has found it necessary to experiment on a much broader scale. To putter around with a single passenger plane is one thing; to accomplish the speedy take-off of large numbers of warships is, of course, quite another.

Once the techniques have been mastered, winter flying in Interior and Arctic Alaska can be performed without much interruption or difficulty. Writing in *Fortune,* Dr. Stefansson stated: "Flying conditions in the Arctic are considerably better than along many of the commercial routes within the United States." The weather is also relatively calm and clear in Alaska's inland regions. In all seasons airplanes ferried to the Soviet Union would find conditions far more favorable by way of Fairbanks and Nome than out past the Aleutians; and they would, according to Dr. Stefansson, find them especially favorable in wintertime. He stated in his *Fortune* article that "every lake is by nature a reasonably good landing field, plenty good enough for experienced Alaskan, Canadian and Siberian flyers. The distance from Chicago to Fairbanks is increased by only 200 or 300 miles if the pilot flies down the Mackenzie along the route used for many years by Mackenzie Air Service and Canadian Airways. That route can be stocked every summer by railway and river steamboat with all the gas and other supplies needed for next winter's ferrying of fighting planes, if they come over in hundreds or thousands. Nature has provided the Arctic with natural landing fields, seaplane bases, and river or ice highways thousands of miles long. The United Nations would be well advised to take advantage of them."

While the flying weather along this inland route is excellent, strategy has dictated that most Army and Navy bases in Alaska be built in the southern coastal region and on the island chain where flying conditions are notoriously bad. Cold is no problem in this region since it is warmed by the Japan Current; January temperatures average 11.2° at Anchorage, 29.8° at Kodiak, 32.2° at Dutch Harbor. The trouble with flying this part of Alaska is that much of the time the coast is shrouded in a thick blanket of fog. It is drenched with rain and wet snows in winter, with drizzling rains in summer. There is heavier precipitation at some points along the Alaskan coast than anywhere in the States.

As described in an aviation bulletin:

Fog may occur at any time . . . Every island and peninsula in the area is mountainous; the tops of many are snow-covered the year around, as well as the long mountain ranges further inland. This feature and the fact that numerous glaciers abound throughout the region enhances rapid cooling of the air as it passes over the mountains, with the ultimate result that low stratus and fog conditions exist for long periods at a time. At other times, the normal nocturnal cooling produces fog which usually forms after midnight and persists until the following noon, or later, unless dispelled by clearing winds or dissipated by surface heating.

When Pan American first began operating to Alaska, it flew a seaplane up the Coast; but it abandoned this the next year and began the operation of wheeled planes along an inland route. The company is highly respected for its resource-

ful pioneering of the United States-Alaska service, and for the
competence of its northland operation. It has never had a
passenger casualty. But no matter how resourceful or how
cautious the company may be, it can hardly get around the
fact that Alaska's capital is located at Juneau, at the foot of
towering mountains on the fog-drenched coast.

Getting out of Juneau, as Joe Crosson conservatively puts
it, is a "problem." The weather may be excellent a short way
inland, but in some seasons Pan American planes are
grounded at Juneau for as much as a week at a time. Day after
day people who thought their friends had "gone Outside,"
see them mournfully downing scotch-and-sodas at the Baranof
bar. The Pan American "suit-case drill" is a joke with sea-
soned Alaskan travelers. Courteously and hopefully, the
agents telephone the passengers bright and early in the morning; politely, they seek them out at the counter of the Baranof
restaurant as they gulp their breakfast coffee; speedily they
rush them in taxis out to the airport, only to see a thick fog
come drifting down over the 6,000-foot mountains to the east.
Sometimes the pilot takes off, without passengers, to look
around. If he is uncertain, the passengers are carted back to
town again to play ping-pong at the Pan American office, or
to slump in disgust on the couches of the Baranof lounge,
until they are again rushed out to the field—perhaps on
another false alarm.

It is with conditions like these that the Army and Navy
have had to cope in developing their coastal bases and air
fields. "Weather reports suspended for the duration," cracked
the Kodiak *Bear* shortly after the war began; "But, Man, this
ain't Pebble Beach!" The *Bear* frequently runs a box at the
top of the front page with the Mark Twain slogan, "If you
don't like the weather, wait a minute."

In one edition the soldiers carried an extensive "technical classification . . . so the newcomers to our garden isle of Alaska will be able to distinguish between the various kinds of rain and mist which are so famous in this land."

Altus Mistus [this story informed its readers] is sometimes called rain, but is strictly a mist. It descends in a translucent cloud and it defies the rain clothes manufacturer inasmuch as it engulfs everything in a thin film of water, very cleansing and refreshing. *Semi-Altus Mistus* is very gratifying to metal manufacturers supplying Kodiak because it necessitates replacements due to oxidation. *Pluvius Williwaws* is a pluvius genteelus combined with a williwaws which whirls the wind in all directions almost at the same time. Very interesting because it keeps the "rain ants" (people out in the rain) guessing as to the velocity and direction of the next blast. *Pluvius General*—a heavy type. During this type of weather, profanity is very prolific and pointed, abuse is rampant and everyone is in good humor because they have a target at which to vent their pent-up bad feelings.

The coastal weather is really no joke. It is dangerous and difficult and ominous, and it is bound to be a determining factor in the fate of Alaska in this war. Skill and experience can go a long way in combating the hazards. As of April, 1942, the veteran pilots of Alaska had flown eighteen months without a single crash. It was a remarkable record—but it was based on caution on the ground as well as on performance in the air. To show that the bad weather conditions are not being exaggerated, it need only be pointed out that until the war, and for several months after it began, none of the lines started a scheduled service along the coast between Juneau, the Territory's capital, and Anchorage, headquarters of the Alaska Defense Command. To get to Anchorage from Juneau it was necessary to take a boat across the Gulf of Alaska and a train up from Seward—a trip of at least three days. Likewise, commercial pilots have long been reluctant in some seasons to fly from Anchorage to the important Navy base at Kodiak.

On the strategic Aleutians the weather is even worse than on the mainland coast. An article in the *Naval Institute Proceedings*, describing the majestic snowcapped Aleutian volcanoes, said of 8,000-foot Mt. Shishaldin: "Unfortunately, on account of the prevalent fog, it is seldom visible, and one traveler passed it a hundred times before seeing it in the clear." At Dutch Harbor, humidity ranges from 70 to 100 per cent the year round, and rain or snow falls 180 days out of the year. Storms and gales make flying even more treacherous. It is along the Aleutians that American fliers may go to execute offensive missions against Japan. It is around these islands that the decisive battles of the North Pacific are likely to be fought.

Yet as described by one veteran flier:

The weather throughout the year may well be classed as bad. The sky is generally overcast and all extremes of weather phenomena except temperatures may be experienced.

Winds often reach gale force, accompanied by widespread precipitation. They have been estimated by residents of this region to exceed 100 miles per hour at times and often last for days.

In view of Alaska's treacherous weather conditions, the government's new airways program is of extraordinary importance. Instrument flying can do much to combat the difficulties. According to Marshall Hoppin: "The Alaskan flying has been hellish—but it is already a thousand per cent easier than it was when we arrived. Upon the completion of our program Alaska will have more good instrument flying weather than some sections of the continental United States."

Joe Crosson seconds this opinion. "Conditions in Alaska,"

he says, "are by no means as difficult as they sound. Our biggest problem was lack of fields and modern flying aids."

When the CAA began its Alaskan program, some of the local fliers made good-natured fun of it. Delivering a load of construction supplies for one of the fields, Pilot Art Woodley was surprised to find that even the temporary landing strip which the CAA had cleared on a nearby river bar was three thousand feet long.

"What do you want to put a field out there for, Hop?" he asked Marshall Hoppin when he returned to Anchorage. "You've already got one. If you build one any larger than that, we're liable to get lost on it."

But every veteran pilot in Alaska knows that the old era of Alaskan aviation is closing, never to return. Most of them do not yet have the equipment or the training to fly over the top on instruments but, practical pioneers that they are, they know what the big fields and beams and weather stations foretell for the future, and they want to keep in step. According to Marshall Hoppin, "the boys want to fly the beams"; a dozen of them have gone out to the States in the past year to get instrument training, and most of the others are preparing to do the same as soon as they can manage it.

Important economic changes as well will be effected by the airways program, and the beginnings of this process are visible even now. Galena, the site of one of the new CAA fields, has grown from a tiny native village to a thriving community—with a roadhouse and a trading post. The same is true at Aniak, where, according to Marshall Hoppin, "everything is going great guns," and Northway is "getting to be quite a little metropolis." Trapping and mining have already been stimulated in the regions around some of the CAA fields hitherto inaccessible because of lack of roads and the short cruising range of the small Alaskan planes.

"Aviation, well planned, could develop Alaska," says Hoppin. He visualizes the large scale use of freighting planes to carry drills to remote mineralized regions, to be followed by construction of roads if the exploratory work proves successful. He also thinks that planes will be the medium whereby Americans will finally come to discover Alaska.

"What will happen to all these bombers and fighters after the war?" he asks. "They'll be turned over to commercial use. As the planes get bigger and bigger, carrying more and more people, the fares will go down. It'll cost only a couple hundred bucks to fly to Alaska. Then maybe it will drop to a hundred. Our new airports will be centers of an enormous tourist trade and economic development. And many of those people will come to Alaska to stay."

But Mr. Hoppin and other northern aviation leaders have even larger visions than this for the region. Ever since Pan American began its experimental flights ten years ago it has been looking forward to the day when it would jump off from Nome and establish a commercial route into Russia and China. The experienced, world-encompassing company has long considered this far northern route an entirely practical one. Almost without exception, round-the-world fliers have gone through Alaska, including the historic Army flight in 1924, the Post and Gatty flight in 1931, the Post flight in 1933 and the record-making Hughes flight in 1938. The people in Fairbanks, who have watched such fliers refuel at their small airport, sense the excitement of the future as few other Americans sense it.

"This," Dr. Charles Bunnell, University of Alaska president, told me proudly, "will some day be a great international aviation center. All you have to do is look at the globe to see that."

Looking ahead to the future, the region is destined to play

an even more important role than that of a way-station to Russia and China. It can become one of the leading air stations of the whole world. Transarctic flights are now an established reality; four of them have already been achieved, one by dirigible, three by plane. According to a Pan American executive in New York, the company developed its Alaskan business not only as a route which might be extended across the North Pacific into Asia, but also "as a practical laboratory for Arctic and future transpolar operations."

Fairbanks lies like the hub of a wheel, amazingly central to the largest aggregations of world civilization. From Fairbanks it is 3,260 miles to New York, 3,510 to Tokyo, 4,110 to Moscow, 4,210 to London, and 4,260 to Berlin. The time may well come when huge, multi-motored ships will thunder down onto the runways of Alaska's towns, and Oriental and European travelers will deplane as casually as fur-capped trappers from Fortymile now climb out of the small, single-motored Bellancas and Stinsons.

"Alaska could radiate millions of airplanes," says Marshall Hoppin; and as you watch his face light up with enthusiasm, you know he means it—to this experienced and capable aviation official such a prospect represents no wild dream, but an entirely practical possibility.

The late General ("Billy") Mitchell's statement that "Alaska is the most important strategic place in the world" has been much quoted, since war began, with reference to the region's proximity to Japan and Russia. Actually, as the full context shows, his meaning covered a great deal more.

"Alaska," he said, "is the most central place in the world of aircraft, and that is true either of Europe, Asia or North America, for whoever holds Alaska will hold the world, and I think it is the most important place in the world."

VI

LIFELINES TO THE NORTH

JAPAN GREATLY DISTURBED OVER PROPOSED HIGHWAY
TO ALASKA FROM U.S., CANADA

The newspaper *Hochi* said today that Japan is greatly disturbed over reported plans for building a military highway from the United States to Alaska through Western Canada.

The newspaper said that the Tokyo foreign office was informed that a string of airbases will be built along the highway by the United States and Canadian governments.

Hochi declared: "American measures in this direction will be regarded as a continuation of the horseshoe-shaped encirclement of Japan by the Washington government. Military bases of the United States would thus be strategic from Singapore, via Australia, the Philippines, Hawaii and the United States to Canada and Alaska."

The western-most islands of the Alaska territory are closer than Hawaii to Japan. The newspaper assumed that the United States would be given joint use of British air bases in the South Seas.

This story appeared in a Seattle newspaper early in 1940, at a time when few Americans knew or cared that a military highway might be built to Alaska. It was not the first time that the Japanese had shown concern over the possibility of an overland route to Alaska. As long as forty years ago, when E. H. Harriman made his proposal for a Canadian-Alaskan railroad to be linked with a projected Russian railroad by a bridge or tunnel at Bering Strait, the Japanese were influential in scotching the plan. By the account of the late J. A. L. Waddell, engineer assigned to the job, the Japanese exacted a verbal agreement at the Portsmouth Conference following the Russo-Japanese War that the Russian part of the system would not be built. Harriman, who had dreamed of linking the American, Asiatic, and European railroad systems, is reported to have declared he would go through with the Canadian-Alaskan part of the road "if it broke the United States." However, his death marked the end of the railroad expansion era, and the project was never revived.

The possibility of an overland connection between the United States and Alaska was discussed in Congress as early as the seventies. In the decades following the failure of the Harriman plan, as the United States' road system developed, suggestions for a highway were made from time to time—but with no results. It took the present war to efface international squabbles and commercial opposition, to jolt the American and Canadian governments into action. At the time the Japanese attacked, Canadian roads and railroads came to a dead-end stop in the wilderness some six hundred miles north of the United States border; and the land beyond to Alaska's major Army bases, a vast scramble of wild forest, big mountain peaks, and deep river valleys, was impassable to anything on wheels. When the history of the past era is written, few aspects of it will seem more curious, more incredible, perhaps more tragic, than the fact that no overland connection to Alaska was built.

The first serious proposal for a highway to Alaska was made in 1928 by an energetic bushy-browed Alaskan engineer, Donald MacDonald. MacDonald, who was the first to detail a practical highway route on a map, had worked on the location and construction of several of the transcontinental railroads before he went north to Alaska. There he spent eight years as chief draftsman and resident and location engineer for the Alaska Railroad, and eighteen years as a locating or exploratory engineer for the Alaska Road Commission. Deciding that there should be an overland route to the States, he began a one-man crusade for the project which he continued doggedly and unsuccessfully down the years.

"Many will regard the proposed highway to Alaska as a dream," he wrote in 1928. "It may be so, but it is no idle dream. The governments of the United States and Canada will profit greatly. The time to begin the work is now."

The *Seward Gateway* ran a special edition on Mr. MacDonald's proposal, and an International Highway Association was formed in Fairbanks, with the slogan, "Seven million dollars purchased Alaska for the States: seven million more will make Alaska one of the United States." Mr. MacDonald prepared the first maps, based on existing information as to terrain, climate, and resources, and the plan attracted the attention of men high in political and industrial life all over North America. A few months later the Interior Department in Washington announced that it was collaborating with the Canadian government on plans for a highway. Bills were introduced in Congress, and in 1930 President Hoover appointed a Commission of engineers to study the project. When their report three years later recommended construction, Congress enacted a law authorizing the President to negotiate with the Canadian government on the matter, but without result.

To Donald MacDonald the highway became an obsession. To prove that a road could be built through the wild, rugged forests and mountains, he made extended exploratory trips across the northland country. Sitting by his lonely campfires, studying his maps, he dreamed of the time when trucks and automobiles would speed across the land through which he was then laboriously breaking his own way without a trail. At first he envisioned the highway as an artery for tourists, and in 1929 his imaginary "motor log," published in the New York *Times,* dazzled American readers with its description of "wildly beautiful primitive country, ancient totem poles, great caribou herds, flashing trout—two thousand miles of scenic wonders." The following year, in his letter to Soviet highway officials proposing that they build a road to Bering Strait, he argued: "There are twenty-five million automobiles in the United States and it would be the ambition of every automobile owner to make this thrilling trip through the wild frontiers of America and Asia into Great Russia and effete Europe. What an effect this should have on international understanding, the dispelling of propaganda-fostered misconceptions and hatreds!" In 1933, the economic collapse gave him a new argument. "The International Highway," he told the American Legion at Fairbanks, "contains the elements for the solution of the depression."

Even then he foresaw the military need for a highway connection. "In the event of an emergency," he warned the Legion, "surface transportation, cutting time two-thirds between the supply depots of the United States and Alaska, may well be a deciding factor." A few years later he wrote an article in *Liberty* magazine entitled, "The Ramparts We Don't Watch," arguing that Alaska, as well as Hawaii, needed defending. "I don't know," he declared, "who taught people to place all their reliance on Pearl Harbor, but I do know their blind faith is not shared in Alaska. We can't afford to let Alaska remain a naval liability, which is exactly what she will be as long as she has no overland connection with the States."

It is remarkable that a project so vital to America should have continued down the years as little more than the obsession of a lone engineer and a small group of his friends in Alaska. Back in 1934, when Donald MacDonald was locating a road in the Copper River country, he met a sourdough trapper, Slim Williams, and they talked about the possibility of a highway down to the States. Later Slim took a dog team over the route, and Donald MacDonald sent him fifty dollars toward the trip. When Slim got to Seattle, he put some motorcycle wheels on his sled. Later he rattled across the country to the Chicago World's Fair, where he met Mrs. Roosevelt. She rode on his sled and later stated: "The outstanding thing I remember about the Fair was the big Alaskan advocate of the International Highway with the far-away look in his eyes." On another occasion Slim, accompanied by John Logan of New York, took a motorcycle over the route to demonstrate its practicability to Assistant Secretary of War Louis Johnson, who had disparaged it.

The Alaska legislature appropriated small amounts of money from time to time to further MacDonald's work, and in 1941 he sent Elden Borders, a University of Alaska student engineer, over the route to investigate snow and other conditions. Borders, who started down on January 21, covered 1,400 miles in ninety-one days and found an average of not over two to two and a half feet of snow throughout the route, with the exception of one pass where it got as deep as five feet.

On one occasion, when the question of Donald MacDonald's funds came up, an Alaskan legislator objected on the ground that he was "not a hundred per cent mentally efficient." It is true that MacDonald, impatient with constant defeats, had pursued his object with fanatical zeal—but, surveying the cold facts of history, it may well be wondered who was mentally efficient—this lone, much-ridiculed Alaskan, or persons in high places in Canada and the United States.

In 1938, five years after the Hoover Commission rendered its report, President Roosevelt appointed a second International Highway Commission consisting of Donald Mac-Donald, Congressman Warren Magnuson of Washington, Governor Gruening of Alaska, Thomas Riggs, ex-Governor, and James Carey, a Seattle engineer. The Canadian government shortly afterward appointed a similar commission headed by the Honorable Charles Stewart, former Premier of Alberta. The two groups conducted aerial and foot reconnaissance surveys of the proposed routes, and both of them found that construction was feasible.

The route recommended by the American Commission, now known as the "A" route, followed a direct line north from Prince George, British Columbia. It ran an average distance of 125 miles from the Coast. It was for the most part the route that Donald MacDonald had proposed in 1928. On the basis of foot reconnaissance by a dozen American and Canadian engineers, the Commission reported that the route lay in "very simple terrain"; that owing to the protection of the high coastal range snow depths would be light, that the road could be kept open in winter more easily than roads in any of the northern states since it lay immediately behind the coastal range in an area of semi-aridity, that a gravel road could be built as a rush job in eighteen months. It would then take only sixty hours to move heavy supplies over this road from Prince George to Fairbanks, compared with the eight days now required by boat and rail from Seattle.

The Canadian Commission, while agreeing that the "A" route was practical, chose a somewhat more easterly "B" route because it was considered to have more possibilities for economic development. Although there was now little question as to the feasibility of a highway, no action followed on these reports. The War Department was lukewarm on the project: in October, 1941, Secretary of War Stimson told the House Roads Committee that construction was considered justified only on a low priority, although it appeared desirable as a "long range defense measure." Delays continued even after the war began, and anyone wandering into Delegate Dimond's office was apt to find Donald MacDonald sitting by himself in a corner, marking routes on British Columbia maps with bright crayons and muttering angrily under his breath. Testifying in February, 1942, he told Congressmen:

"Not only is an empire at stake, not only are a valiant frontier people threatened with all the horrors that have already occurred in the Pacific, but we run the risk of losing the world's most strategic area from which a foul enemy may dominate all of North America.

"Time is pressing. Let it not be said of us, as it has been said too frequently of others, 'Too little and too late.'"

The following month construction of a road to Alaska was announced. In an exchange of notes between Jay Pierrepont Moffat, United States Minister in Ottawa, and Canadian Prime Minister W. L. Mackenzie King, it was agreed that the United States would survey and build the road and maintain it during the emergency; that Canada would acquire the rights of way, waive charges incident to the construction, and make construction material available; and that the Canadian part of the road would revert to Canada after the war, on proviso that it be open to United States civilian traffic without discrimination. The United States Army, it was agreed, would build it hastily as a "pioneer road," to be converted into a more permanent artery at a later date by the United States Public Roads Administration.

Suddenly it was a matter of days, not years. United States

Engineer troops were rushed north to the Dawson Creek rail-head, north of the State of Washington, to fell the first timber, build the first bridges, and begin the cutting of a desperately needed road toward the North. Arriving by the thousands, they worked twenty-four hours a day, seven days a week, racing to get their supplies in before the spring thaw. The crews laid sawdust on Peace River to preserve the ice. Big, six-wheeled trucks clattered over hastily constructed plank bridges and jolted their supplies along an old fur-trading trail through deep forest and over frozen muskeg to the Fort Nelson Airport. Maps of the land beyond indicated few names; for it had been traversed by the Hudson's Bay trappers and the '98 gold rush boomers—but by few others.

At last a road was to be built to Alaska—or so it was universally hoped. It should have been a great day for Donald MacDonald; but he was plunged into gloom—and this time he was not alone. Although the Army hoped to complete the road within the year, it was feared by many persons of authority, including Alaska's Governor Ernest Gruening, Delegate Dimond, and qualified engineers generally familiar with the northland terrain, that this was out of the question. The route chosen by the Army, known as the "C" route, was not the one recommended by the Alaskan International Highway Commission on the basis of their four years of engineering surveys. Nor had the Army Engineers had a part in the selection. The choice was affected by a prior decision of the Canadian-American Joint Defense Board, organization of Army and Navy officials, of which Fiorello La Guardia is chairman. Lying some 400 miles inland, the route followed the line of new military air fields built under the auspices of the Joint Defense Board at Fort St. John, Fort Nelson, Watson Lake, intermediate points between Edmonton and Whitehorse. The Army was using these new fields to fly its war planes north to Alaska. Lacking any overland connection, the new fields at Fort Nelson and Watson Lake were supplied, at the time, solely by air.

The reasons advanced for the choice of the route were the necessity of linking up the new air fields and of placing the road inland so it would not be so vulnerable to attack. However, it had never been surveyed, except by air. The first part of it passed through difficult muskeg country, and beyond that it crossed the height of land, a plateau-like region at the junction of the Stikine and Rocky Mountains and the Coast range. The terrain conditions were so little known and so forbidding that many persons feared the road would not reach Alaska in time to be useful in this war.

As soon as the Alaskan International Highway Commission heard the news of the decision, they wired President Roosevelt:

WE ARE DELIGHTED TO HEAR THROUGH THE PRESS THAT THE ROAD TO ALASKA IS TO BECOME A REALITY AND THAT THE ARMY HAS BELATEDLY ACCEPTED THE VIEW WHICH YOUR COMMISSION HAS BEEN URGING UPON IT FOR SEVERAL YEARS. HOWEVER WE KNOW THAT THE ARMY IS MAKING A SERIOUS BLUNDER IN THE SELECTION OF THE ROUTE IF IT IS TO BE BUILT AS REPORTED AND WOULD STRONGLY URGE THAT YOU REQUEST THE ARMY TO CONFER WITH THIS COMMISSION WHICH HAS STUDIED THE SUBJECT THOROUGHLY FOR FOUR YEARS. THE ROUTE REPORTED TO HAVE BEEN SELECTED BY THE ARMY CAN NOT POSSIBLY BE BUILT WITHIN THE TIME LIMIT SUPPOSEDLY ANNOUNCED BY IT

The layman felt no disposition to question a military decision in wartime, but it was disturbing to learn that the choice was also questioned in Canada.

According to a New York *Times* Ottawa dispatch: "Among

engineers and others who have given serious study to the problem of the Alaska Highway during many years, there is much serious misgiving here regarding the decision that has been taken in Washington in favor of the route northwest from the Peace River country across Yukon to Whitehorse."

The Honorable George Black, former speaker of the Canadian House of Commons, also warned against the length of time it would take to build over the "C" route and the Ottawa *Times* declared editorially:

Official Canada is in the delicate position of being unable to urge reconsideration of the Washington decision as the United States is to pay the whole cost of the work. . . . It is in a spirit of good neighbor, with no axe to grind and no motive but to serve the interest of North America's contribution to winning the war, that this unofficial point of view is submitted. It is known that the Alaska highway can be built to serve the desired military purpose over one of the routes recommended by the Highway Commission. The decision to start building over unknown territory may mean serious delay.

While the length of new construction required over the two routes did not differ appreciably, the "A" route recommended by the American and Canadian Highway Commissions presented no comparable obstacles of terrain, either of muskeg or of mountain, and low-grade roads, rivers, and lakes paralleled it for over seven hundred miles. This fact alone would render the construction job far simpler than over the more remote "C" route.

Whether or not the "C" route would contribute to the winning of the war, it would contribute very measurably to the fortunes of the Canadian Pacific Railway, long a potent factor in Canadian politics. Not only would the "C" route give the company more of the long-haul business from the

East, but Canadian Pacific had recently bought control of Yukon Southern Air Transport Ltd., "bush" line that flew the inland air route along which the new military fields were constructed. (No American company is allowed to establish a commercial airline over this route.) Canadian Pacific also stood to gain since it operates a steamship line to Alaska, with which the more westerly "A" route would compete to a far greater extent.

Testifying before a Senate Foreign Relations sub-committee, Brigadier General C. L. Sturdevant, Assistant Chief of Army Engineers, stated that the "C" route had been chosen "for the purpose of connecting the air fields." Lieutenant Colonel F. Brewer of the Air Corps Ferry Command stated: "Gasoline has to be put in at Watson Lake and Fort Nelson, and there is no way of putting it in there now except to fly it in. We want the road to go that way."

No one questioned the need for an overland connection between the new military air fields. The only query in critics' minds was how fast the route could be developed into an effective supply line for Alaska, and it was apparent that speed had not been the primary consideration in the choice of the "C" route.

As the conflict sharpened in the North Pacific, suddenly the question was not whether to build an overland connection to Alaska, but how many to build, and what kind. As late as July, 1942, Delegate Dimond introduced a bill for immediate construction along the "A" route. At the same time, Dr. Stefansson, writing in the July issue of *Fortune,* urged development of still another means of supply to the North. *1942*

A generation that tends to think lazily in terms of railroads, ships, and trucks has almost forgotten the value of river highways. In North America the Mackenzie River, second only to the

Mississippi system, is the historic commercial highway of north-western Canada. It begins to be navigable at the head of rail north of Edmonton, and flows almost straight in the direction of Japan and China. The Mackenzie does not go to the Bering Sea, but the Yukon River does: and the Yukon is the third longest river highway of the North American continent. It could be coordinated with the Mackenzie and the two rivers used practically as one. For the Mackenzie, 300 miles from its delta, is only 300 miles from the head of navigation of the Yukon. All that is needed is to cross a low divide, and the Yukon will carry forward the transport to the Bering Sea. Construction of a road across the divide would give us a 3,000 mile highway extending in the direction of Asia—in summer a liquid highway for steamboats, and in winter an automotive road paved level and hard with ice. This is actually a more essential project than the construction of the Alaska Highway.

Proponents of the road link between rivers declared it could be built in six weeks as soon as the freeze-up came, and claimed that this was the only route that could be completed in time for use this year. They also pointed out that it would facilitate petroleum supply from Canada to Alaska. Feasibility of Stefansson's river scheme was also a subject of controversy, but in any case it did not supplant the need for an effective overland supply to Alaska—since there were several months during the spring break-up and fall freeze-up when the rivers could not be used.

Another proposal was made—for a railroad—and this gained powerful Administration and Army backing. Soon after the first Army Engineer troops were rushed up to begin work on route C, other groups of Army engineers were dispatched north to begin surveys for a railroad along the "B" route, beginning, like the "A" route, at the Canadian National Railroad terminal at Prince George, and running north between the other two as far as the Yukon border, then swerving away from them in a more easterly route toward Fairbanks. Even this route was the subject of controversy, but its backers claimed it was the best way for a railroad, following easy water grades most of the way north.

It was reported that the Administration, as well as outstanding Army supply chiefs, now favored a railroad because its large-scale transportation units would handle more efficiently, in both winter and summer, the large volume of men and supplies that it might be necessary to move overland to Alaska. For example, if it should become necessary to supply 300,000 troops in Alaska, according to unofficial estimates, some 10,000 tons of material would be required every twenty-four hours. Standard locomotives could easily haul this tonnage with less than fifteen trains of only thirty cars each, and it was estimated that modern locomotives of the Consolidated type, with a working load of 45,000 pounds on each axle, could haul the load over this route with as few as nine trains every twenty four hours.

It was not easy for the layman to evaluate the various plans and proposals, especially when so little was known about much of the terrain involved, over which engineers themselves were in dispute. But as the war developed, it did not take a military or engineering expert to realize one thing— that supply to Alaska had become a life and death matter to the cause of the United Nations, that blunders and delays were now unthinkable, that prompt, decisive action in this matter was one of the steps urgently needed for the winning of the war.

Author's Note: The Army engineers, working day and night on one of the most spectacular construction jobs in American history, have done much to make up for the delays and blunderings of the past; and, late in September, Secretary of War Stimson announced that the highway would be ready for use as a winter road by December 1, 1942.

VII

LAND WITHOUT PEOPLE

THE PIONEERS' HOME at Sitka, where sourdoughs spend their last days at the expense of the Territory, stands across the water from the Navy air base. As these oldtimers rock back and forth in their sitting rooms, they gossip ceaselessly about the Klondike or Fortymile or Nome. "There is more gold mined in that building than all the rest of the Territory," one Sitkan wisecracked. But in recent years, these men have had some new topics for discussion.

They have seen a steady procession of red trucks tearing through the muddy street with loads of sand and gravel, a steady line of motorboats crossing the channel with loads of uniformed troops. They have heard the roar of Navy patrol planes and seen small fishing boats rocked by dredging operations. Their windows have rattled with the thunder of dynamite blasts, and when a sentry fired a shot at one of the local fishermen who drifted into the Navy reserve, it was as much as some of them could take.

"The old Alaska is gone," one white-headed prospector complained, as he rocked back and forth with a gold nugget dangling from his watch-chain. "She's wrecked. This is about as bad as being invaded by the enemy."

It was not bad for the small-town merchants, however. As contractors got busy on $200,000,000 worth of defense work, as thousands of high-paid construction workers arrived to

88

build the bases, the Territory's towns experienced a boom surpassing that of the old Gold Rush. In one year deposits in small banks near the bases more than tripled. The volume of liquor sales, always large in Alaska, rose fast. Rents skyrocketed. Travelers were always worried about finding accommodations. (When I arrived in Juneau, the Baranof Hotel had no rooms vacant and I slept on a cot just off the lobby in the banquet hall.) New hotels opened; but sometimes they had to crowd several cots into one room to take care of their customers. At Sitka the jail accommodated transients for three dollars a night.

Prices rose steeply everywhere. Asked how the Alaskans had received the troops, an Army officer replied: "With an open hand—palm up." Soldiers complained that an Anchorage drugstore that used to charge ten cents for a coke raised the price to fifteen in off-hours, and in rush hours boosted it to twenty. Out at Kodiak the *Bear* commented: "Thirty-five cents is a hell of a lot to pay for a hamburger sandwich and they sock you sixty cents for a two-bit drink."

For a while ice ran so short in Anchorage that it brought eighty dollars a ton. The local telephone company had so much business it refused to take orders for new installations. It was a nice thing. It was a nice thing, too, for the Alaska Railroad, which hauled so much lumber and steel and coal and ammunition and other supplies that it showed a $2,500,000 profit after long years of deficits; and for Eustace P. Ziegler, Alaskan painter, who sold a hundred of his vividly colored oil landscapes in four months. Even the government's famous agricultural colony at Matanuska was affected by the boom. While some of the farmers got busy producing milk and butter for the Army, many others drifted off to take high-paying construction jobs at the bases. As the war progressed, and the gold and salmon industries were crippled for lack of machinery and boats, many of the Alaskans were to see hard times. But the Territory's merchants experienced a boom such as they had never known.

And yet this boom was only a repetition of a time-worn Alaskan pattern—the pattern of an unstable economy and a floating population. Throughout its history Alaska has been swept by hordes of transients.

First there were the Russian explorers and hunters of the seventeenth and eighteenth centuries. Their take was fur—the fox and sea otter and seal that swarmed along the Aleutian and Bering Sea islands. In the latter days of Russian rule the Czar's Russian American Company managed the fur trade and engaged in many other activities in Alaska—building ships, casting church bells and operating sawmills.

When the United States bought the Territory, it fell into neglect. The Alaska Commercial Company was given a charter to take over the fur-seal monopoly, but for the most part the region lay stagnant, until the Gold Rush stirred it into a new burst of economic activity. During this chaotic and violent era, lucky stampeders took out their precious metal and departed, leaving many ghost towns behind.

Those were the major cataclysms. There were also lesser ones. Shortly after the turn of the century a J. P. Morgan-Guggenheim "Syndicate" bought extensive Alaskan mining and fishing interests. Their Kennecott mines in the Copper River and Latouche regions employed several thousand men over a period of years, producing over $200,000,000 worth of metal. Then, having worked out their best ore, these mines closed down, leaving much desolation and many relief cases in the nearby towns. In a 1940 editorial entitled, "Alaska for Alaskans," the Cordova *Times* asked:

Does it mean that financial octopi in the States are to be permitted to flick a tentacle into the Alaskan hills, suck up its quick wealth, and withdraw, leaving that immediate section of the country in a precarious situation? . . . Alaska for Alaskans should mean that the Territory's latent resources be developed so there would be more of Alaska for more Alaskans.

After three-quarters of a century under American rule Alaska has virtually no population. By the last census the number of people living in the entire region, including both natives and whites, was less than 73,000—not quite enough to fill the Yale Bowl. Since then, the population (exclusive of troops) has increased to about 80,000. If this number were evenly dispersed throughout the region, there would be only one person to every seven and a half square miles.

This is a fact of military importance, and one of the Territory's gravest weaknesses in time of war. It means that the Army and Navy have had to fend for themselves. There were almost no civilians to supply them with goods and services. There are almost no Alaskans to aid them by guerrilla fighting in the event of an enemy attack. A few forward-looking officials in Washington had warned for years that the Territory's sparse population was a dangerous strategic weakness. When the government established its agricultural colony at Matanuska in 1935, this was one of the factors it had in mind, but nothing was done beyond that.

If the country were the frozen waste that many people think it is, its sparsely populated condition would be understandable and would afford less cause for alarm. But this is not the case. Alaska has been a land of transients. But it is a land *for* pioneers.

The word "Alaska," by some accounts, comes from a native term, "Al-ay-ek-sa," meaning "The Great Land." In more ways than one the country does full credit to the name. Tourists passing through Alaska are staggered by its gigantic, almost fearful splendor, and Henry Gannett, former Chief Geographer of the United States Geological Survey, once declared: "Nowhere else in the earth is there such abundance and magnificence of mountain fjord and glacier scenery. . . . For the one Yosemite of California, Alaska has hundreds. The mountains and glaciers of the Cascade Range are duplicated and a thousand times exceeded in Alaska. The Alaska Coast is to become the show place of the earth; and pilgrims, not only from the United States but from far beyond the seas, will throng in endless procession to see it."

Sportsmen like Colonel "Wild Bill" Donovan, General Robert Wood and Nelson Rockefeller also found Alaska great —for it has some of the largest herds of big game left in the world, and some of the animals themselves are unsurpassed in size. The brown bears that lumber along the salmon streams of the southeastern islands, Kodiak, and the Alaska Peninsula are the biggest carnivorous animals on earth, with mammoth heads measuring up to "eleven axe-handles" across; and on the Kenai Peninsula, Alaska has three or four thousand of the biggest moose in the world, with majestic antler spreads up to eighty-one inches.

The Army and Navy also found Alaska great—too great in terms of size and what they had to accomplish in a short time. But they had little occasion to discover the greatness of its undeveloped resources. From the account of their difficulties in fortifying Alaska it might seem that the region is a forbidding, unproductive waste. But most of their trouble, as General Buckner stated, was caused by lack of transportation facilities and by the fact that Alaska was still a near-wilderness.

As heavily laden transports steamed past the thick spruce forests, few of the soldiers realized that big newsprint mills could be built along these shores. As bombers and pursuits flew across the rugged mountain ranges on patrol, few of the pilots thought about the wealth of unexplored minerals hidden beneath the rocky slopes. As war workers struggled to construct fortifications on frozen subsoil, few of them knew or cared about the fact that summer crops flourish in the top layer of earth above this permanent frost.

Thus, although in one sense the military builders "discovered" Alaska more extensively than it had ever been discovered before, in many ways they did not discover it at all.

Many years ago the late Dr. Alfred Brooks, for many years head of the Alaska branch of the United States Geological Survey, published a comparison of Alaskan and Scandinavian resources. He knew the region well. He had spent years exploring and mapping it, and it has been said that "there were only two who knew the truth about Alaska's resources—Providence and Dr. Brooks."

The area of Alaska [he wrote] is three times that of Sweden and four times that of Finland. If we compare the agricultural lands, we find that there are much larger areas than in either Sweden or Finland. The mineral resources of Alaska are greater than those of northern Europe. It also has water power comparable with either Sweden or Finland. . . . From the standpoint of both resources, and climate, we are justified in believing that Alaska will maintain a population per square mile at least as great as that of Finland. In fact, we may confidently expect that the time will come when Alaska will support a population of ten million people.

Since Dr. Brooks made this statement, it has become a catchword for government economists trying to develop

Alaska. Some critics have questioned the validity of the Scandinavian comparison. They have pointed out the proximity of those Scandinavian countries to large European markets, which Alaska lacks, and the high living standards of American as compared with Scandinavian farmers. A few have challenged it in terms of climate; but for the most part the criticisms have to do with the above-mentioned social and economic factors and not with any defects within Alaska itself.

To appreciate Alaska it is first of all necessary to understand its climate. Alaskan climate is paradoxical and not easy to comprehend. The first thing you learn is what the Chambers of Commerce tell you—that less than 4 per cent of the region is permanently covered with ice and snow; that three-quarters of it lies in the North Temperate Zone, and that the whole southern coastal stretch, warmed by the Japan Current, has mild winter temperatures.

This coastal region, however, is by no means the warmest part of Alaska all year round. The sea tempers the summers, too, and they are cooler than the summers of the inland regions. That is why most of the permanent ice and snow that does exist in Alaska is found on the jagged mountains and glaciers of this southern region. That is why passengers, sailing along Alaska's shores, are dazzled by the sight of bright blue lupin and pink fireweed fringing the edge of the sea against a backdrop of the eternal winter of white snowcaps.

By contrast the vast Interior region of Alaska, protected from the sea, gets very hot in summer (record: 90° above) just as it gets bitter cold in winter. There are some unorthodox things to learn about the Interior's climate too. Hot as the summers are, the subsoil under the insulating tundra is permanently frozen. Yet when the upper layer of this soil is thawed, these very areas represent some of the best agricultural land in Alaska—far better than in the so-called "temperate" southeast coast where flowers grow luxuriantly, but the climate is too moist for farming. In the hot, dry Interior region plants shoot up high from the few feet of thawed soil and grow prodigiously in the long hours of summer daylight. As you fly over inland and northern Alaska in summer the vast tundra country below you glows emerald-green, puddled with blue rivers and lakes.

Well, you think, at least the northern parts of Alaska would be a good place to live in summer. This is true; but the people who do live there happen to enjoy the sub-zero winter, too. Many of them prefer it. Several women in Fairbanks told me that winter is their favorite season, and a census of school children taken at Nome some years ago showed a 75 per cent preference for winter. Even the far Arctic, according to Dr. Stefansson, is a good place to live and a potentially productive region.

"When the world was once known to be round," Dr. Stefansson wrote over twenty years ago in his book "The Friendly Arctic," "there was no difficulty in finding many navigators to sail around it. When the polar regions are once understood to be friendly and fruitful, men will quickly and easily penetrate their deepest recesses."

In terms of present-day Alaska the vision of Dr. Stefansson and Dr. Brooks seems as grandiose, as remote as the Northern Lights that streak the skies above the northland's lonely tundra. Compared with what it could be, Alaska is still a land without a people. It is still little more than a stamping ground for transients. Today, the Alaskan economy rests insecurely on only two industries of any size—gold and salmon, both of them largely absentee-owned and highly seasonal.

Much of Alaska's labor is migratory and as a result Alaska's per capita wealth production is one of the highest in the world. Today's economic activity is subject to a regularized ebb and flow, conducted in large part by non-residents who remain in the Territory only during the summer months. Every spring, soon after the breakup of the ice on the Yukon River, Alaska is stampeded by miners and cannery workers from the States. The Nenana Ice Pool, in which thousands of Alaskans place bets on the exact second of the breakup, is not only a colorful Territorial tradition, but a highly significant one. Every fall the migrants leave again.

As described by Cap Lathrop, sourdough millionaire: "The trouble is, people just regard Alaska as a treasure box. They want to make their stake and then, when Jack Frost strikes, they all go Out." Governor Ernest Gruening compares the men who make money in Alaska with the seventeenth century Spaniards, who came to the Americas to gather wealth, contrasting them with the Pilgrims who came to settle and develop the country.

Salmon is Alaska's leading product. The Territory produces more than 80 per cent of the nation's total output, and in 1941 over $50,000,000 worth of pinks and reds and cohos and chums were taken out of the waters along its winding, indented shores. For the most part this money was earned back in the States by such companies as Pacific American Fisheries of Bellingham, Washington; Libby, McNeill and Libby of Chicago; and Nakat Packing Corporation and P. E. Harris of Seattle. Much of the labor was "absentee," too; of the twenty thousand workers normally employed, over half migrate north for the summer, returning to the States in the fall. Most of the hiring is done in Seattle under contracts between the companies and C.I.O. and A.F. of L. unions. In the past Alaskans have complained, with good cause, that they were not receiving their due share of the fisheries jobs. In 1939 the salmon industry paid nearly twice as much to non-residents as it did to Alaskans, and Alaskan Indians earned only 13 per cent of the total payroll.

Although to a lesser degree, the $24,000,000 gold industry is also largely seasonal and absentee-owned. There are a few lode mines operating the year round; the largest is Alaska Juneau (headquarters in San Francisco) whose many-tiered mill stands on the steep mountainside behind the Territory's capital town. However, more than two-thirds of Alaska's gold output comes from placer mines which can be operated for only a few months in summer. Most of these are in the vast Interior region, where roads are scarce. There are numerous small operators, most of whom use draglines and bulldozers. However, as the most accessible deposits are worked out, rendering mechanized equipment more and more essential to profitable operation, the small prospecting miner is becoming increasingly rare. A large part of the entire placer output is produced by United States Smelting, Refining and Mining Company, with headquarters in Boston, which operates some of the biggest dredges in the world in the permanently frozen ground around Fairbanks and Nome.

It takes only fifteen men to operate one of these screeching, groaning mechanical giants; but the company employs nearly nine hundred workers at the peak of the summer season, using them in its powerhouse and shops and out on the creeks, where they strip and thaw the ground for the dredging operation. According to the company's manager, Roy Earling, at least half these men go back to the States every fall, returning the following spring. So do a great many of the smaller operators. In the late fall, when the days begin to shorten, the

miners wander into Fairbanks from the creeks and begin to
"go Out."

This annual trek is as familiar to Interior Alaskans as the
migrations of caribou that cross the inland back country by
the thousands every fall. As trainload after trainload of
miners creaks and rattles down through frozen swamp and
mighty snowcaps toward the sea, the men crowd together
along the aisles of the dilapidated railroad cars, playing cards,
telling jokes, drinking, and breaking into loud laughter and
song. Their pockets are full of money, and they are in a care-
less mood, as the Anchorage Hotel can testify from experience. It has two cedar closets full of business suits left by
miners arriving in the spring on their way in to the creeks.
Over a hundred of these suits have been unclaimed for years—
their owners did not bother to stop for them on the way Out.

These suits are a symbol of the transient nature of Alaska's
population. On the way up on the boat, one construction
worker remarked: "I'm going to jail to run up a bank account." Up to the time of the Pearl Harbor attack construction workers left some of the dreary Alaskan bases almost as
fast as they arrived. This attitude has dominated Alaska's life
for decades. According to a leading Territorial official, "It
wasn't till the government built a Federal building in Fairbanks that people began to think about putting in bathtubs."
According to Governor Gruening: "Alaska still has too much
of the atmosphere of the mining camp. The man who comes
to Alaska wants to hang his hat on a nail, make some money,
and get out."

Few people stay to settle and develop Alaska. Little attempt
has been made by the government, or anyone else, to make
Alaska self-sufficient. A symbol of the Alaskan economy is the
can of condensed milk that sits on every counter. Some of the

old sourdoughs dislike fresh eggs, preferring the cold-storage variety shipped up from the States "because they have a snap to them." These are small matters, but they tell a big story. Alaska, despite the wealth of its resources, produces almost nothing for its own needs. Almost everything the Alaskans eat, wear, and work with is imported from the States.

In view of Alaska's isolation by land and the vulnerability of the water route, this is a perilous situation in wartime. It is especially perilous in terms of food. Not only does the Army lack a civilian population to aid it in possible combat; it is worried about feeding the few people who are there. Authorities have urged them to hoard stocks of groceries, and the danger of food shortages was one factor in the evacuation of women and children of Army and Navy personnel and construction workers from Alaska as well as the island possessions.

Vegetables and dairy products are produced at the government's Matanuska Colony near Anchorage, and at a few scattered farms in other regions, but the amount is still negligible in terms of the Territory's food requirements. It is estimated that Alaska annually imports nearly $5,000,000 worth of food and dairy products that it is capable of raising itself. Of an estimated 64,000,000 acres of range and farmland, fewer than 10,000 acres are worked. The Alaskans like to joke about the fact that some of the salmon taken from their own waters is canned, shipped down to Seattle, and then shipped up again. Many Alaskans, as a matter of fact, are so accustomed to imported products that they tend to look askance at anything produced locally. Although some excellent vegetables are produced on Alaskan farms, you have to taste them yourself to be sure—so many Alaskans will tell you they are no good.

The fuel supply situation is similar. Coal represents an out-standing exception to the rule—there are several local mines and their output has increased greatly with the war program, but all the southeastern towns find it cheaper to use oil, ship-ping it up from the States. Alaska itself is believed to contain vast oil deposits, including 11,000,000 acres of land in remote Arctic regions, which the Navy has set aside as a Petroleum Reserve. But to date, even in the more accessible regions, only a few drillings have been attempted although a small well at Katella is producing a few barrels of high-grade oil a day. The situation may be relieved by supply from Canada. As quoted in a recent article by Richard Finnie, the Canadian Minister of Munitions and Supply stated last May in the House of Commons: "Arrangements have been made to de-velop further the wells on the lower Mackenzie at Fort Norman. Additional wells are being drilled, the refinery capacity being increased, and a short pipe line is being in-stalled to bring the oil across to the location of the Alaska highway [Route C]."

Alaska's deep southeastern spruce and hemlock forests con-tain three to four million acres of commercial timber. There are a few small sawmills in the southeastern port towns. These, too, have boomed with the war—turning out some lumber for the bases and spruce for trainer planes. The gov-ernment has also embarked on a large-scale airplane spruce program, and plans to take 100,000,000 board feet of high-grade timber a year out of the southeastern forests, towing it south to Seattle in rafts. However, in normal times the local sawmills' output is small, and there is not enough wood taken from Alaska's forests to supply the Alaska Railroad with ties. The road imports at least half its annual require-ments.

Most Americans have scarcely been aware of Alaska's existence, but the same cannot be said for the city of Seattle, through whose port some $45,000,000 worth of Alaska-bound cargo passes in an average year. If you go down the steep streets to the Alaska Steam dock, wandering up and down among the jumble of cartons and packing boxes, you will realize vividly what Alaska means to the United States in cold, cash terms. Traveling north on one boat there were transformers from Fruitvale, California, for the Ketchikan Public Utilities. Work shirts from Paris, Tennessee, for Koslosky at Anchorage. Tractors from Peoria, Illinois, for the Lytle and Green Construction Company at Valdez. Snuff from Chicago for the West Coast Grocery at Juneau. A desk from Herkimer, New York, for the postmaster at Wrangell. A skiff from Everett, Washington, for a native at Holy Cross. Book matches from San Francisco, for Kodiak. Dog food from St. Paul, Minnesota, for Cordova. Wallboard from Jarratt, Virginia, for Fairbanks.

The street running past Seattle's docks is appropriately named, "Alaskan Way," and in nearby Pioneer Square there stands a huge totem pole, erected in 1897 to commemorate Seattle's role in the development of the Territory. Nearby curio shops are full of Eskimo ivory work, glacier postcards and smaller totems. The *Alaska Weekly,* most widely distributed Territorial newspaper, is published in Seattle, as is the magazine, *Alaska Life.* Seattle is the trade center of Alaska. Most men doing an extensive business in the region maintain offices there and many live there in wintertime. Cap Lathrop maintains an office in Seattle. Pan American's Alaska division has headquarters there, and Joe Crosson lives there much of the year. Glenn Carrington, prominent Fairbanks mining-equipment dealer, winters in Seattle, and the Northern Commercial Company—"Alaska's Pioneer Merchants"—has its headquarters there.

You can learn a great deal about the Alaskan economy simply by stepping into the Northern Commercial office and chatting with its president, white-headed Volney Richmond. The N.C. Company, as the firm is known in Alaska, originated as a small Yukon trading post in the last century. Today it has twenty-eight Alaskan branches at widely scattered settlements like Aniak, Black River, Mission, Ophir, Takotna, and Unalaska, as well as in the larger centers, and branches in several towns in nearby Yukon Territory.

The company does a $5,000,000 business selling everything from caterpillar tractors to calico. On one occasion it received an order from a thrifty Alaskan, trying to save on freight costs, for "a sow that will have pigs about the Fourth of July." This particular transaction came to an unhappy close: Alaska Steam billed the man for a whole litter of pigs, and the sow died en route. But the N.C. Company seeks to oblige its customers on a great variety of orders, and its trade is probably one of the least routine in America. It does a good brokerage business outfitting miners with bunks, food, and clothing for their annual summer migration, and when Pan American pioneered its Juneau to Fairbanks route, the N.C. Company "fixed up" its radio operators' cabins with lanterns, guns, hunting knives, and other essentials.

Owing to the Northland's scarcity of local capital, the company has not stuck to the store business alone. It has drifted into some strange and diversified operations, running the utility system at Fairbanks and the wharfs at Unalaska, and managing small-boat transportation on the lower Yukon.

Alaska is a salesman's country. Traveling through the Territory, you encounter the same faces again and again on the boats and planes and in the lobbies of the small hotels: the man from Stetson Hat, the man from the Great Northern Railway, the man from Burroughs Adding Machine, the perennial flock of grocery representatives. Even the Encyclopædia Britannica regularly sends a salesman to the Territory. (He reports that the Alaskans purchase his volumes much more readily than people in the States.) Sears, Roebuck and Montgomery Ward also do a rousing business in Alaska—and as the war boom developed, their offices in the towns near the bases looked like railroad stations on a holiday. Up at Fairbanks, 45 per cent of the advertising over the local radio station is for national products. Trappers and traders in the remote regions listen over their small battery sets to the latest catch slogans for Standard Oil, Chase and Sanborn Coffee, Fuller paints, Winchester and Remington guns, Wood sleeping bags, and Lipton's Tea.

Transportation charges, added to all prices in Alaska, make living costs very high. According to a 1939 survey made by the American Federation of Federal Employes, it cost 35 per cent more to live in Ketchikan than in Washington, D. C.; and as you proceed north and inland, adding the steep Alaska Railroad tariff to that of the steamship company, prices steadily increase. Up at Fairbanks living costs are over twice as high as in Washington. The local newspaper sells for ten cents, the barber shops charge a dollar for a haircut, and one lunch counter bills you forty cents for a bowl of Campbell's soup. Always: "It's the freight." Anything less than a quarter is seldom seen in the remote settlements of the Interior, and merchandise sold in Alaska is usually high grade, since it does not pay to bring in the cheaper brands. While the government has urged settlers to come to Alaska ("The Newest Homeland") it advises prospective pioneers that they will save little by buying secondhand machinery for shipment to Alaska and asks them not to head north unless they have at least $2,500 on hand. Seasonal wages are good and transients are little bothered by the high prices: but all this has hardly encouraged permanent settlement and development.

Why has Alaska remained a country without a people? In talking with many of the officials and small entrepreneurs who have tried to develop the Territory's resources, I found that the most frequently mentioned obstacles were social and economic and had very little to do with the productivity of the country itself. Transportation costs were considered a major barrier, and, as one authority put it: "The main thing wrong with Alaska's resources is the undeveloped wealth back in the States."

It has been estimated that Alaska has billions of tons of low-grade coal deposits, but there has been practically no interest in this volume because of the unlimited amount unmined back home. Its possible oil deposits have attracted little attention, when there is still a vast reserve in the States. When reindeer meat was introduced on the dining cars of western railroads, the cattle interests raised such an uproar that it was withdrawn. The same kind of obstacle is holding back Alaska's greatest single untapped resource—the spruce and hemlock forests along its southeastern shore. Only as Canadian timberlines are worked farther back will there be a chance of developing Alaska's commercial timber—most of which lies less than three miles from tidewater, with an abundance of cheap power nearby. These forests could yield a million tons of newsprint a year—one-fourth of the United States' needs—and, if developed, would support over thirty thousand people (more than a third of the Territory's present population) in a year-round industry—Alaska's foremost need.

Back in the twenties the Zellerbach interests and a group of California publishers signed preliminary contracts to build Alaskan newsprint plants, but they were cancelled in the depth of the depression, and since then the United States paper industry has made no move to return.

The same kind of shadow falls over its strategic minerals, although in this case the government knows less about what Alaska has to offer. It knows that promising deposits exist, but their quality and the amount and cost of extraction are things it has never spent very much to determine. Chromite, antimony, tungsten, and tin are being surveyed and mined in small amounts; and the Alaska Juneau gold mine has a contract to process 500 tons of chrome ore a day. Large quantities of high-grade iron ore have been discovered, and there has been considerable talk of its possible use to supply a new Pacific electro-metallurgical industry. Nickel and quicksilver are being investigated. Funds for strategic minerals exploration have been much increased in the past few years, but it will be some time before actual production can result, and the first emphasis of the government's program has been placed on the location of more accessible deposits in the States.

Much of this is understandable, but it is difficult to comprehend the failure to develop agriculture, for which there is a local market. There are special problems to be worked out—among them the difficulties of new, patchy soil and the short growing season, but the obstacles most frequently cited by those familiar with the situation are again economic and social. The relatively high seasonal pay of the gold and salmon industries is one of the frequently mentioned factors. As expressed by one man: "Why should a man fool around with a bunch of cows when he can make ten dollars a day at gold mining?" Many others said: "The merchants get commissions from the States. They don't want to fool around with an infant industry."

High costs were blamed by many, who criticized the steamship and railroad rates as exorbitant. "It's a set-up," many Alaskans told me. "Do you think the steamship lines want Alaska to be self-sufficient?" In 1939 the legislature passed a memorial protesting against the steamship rates, but they have been substantially increased since; and, as described later, the steep rates on the Alaska Railroad are not an encouragement to local enterprise.

Government economists have made many studies of Alaskan possibilities, including a National Resources Committee report published in 1937 ("Alaska, Its Resources and Development"), and an Interior Department report in 1939 ("The Problem of Alaskan Development"). Congressional hearings have been held, too, most recently on a bill sponsored by Secretary Ickes to encourage an influx of refugees into the Territory. Great prospects have been outlined for Alaska—but accomplishment to date has been pitifully small.

The Territory is still so much a land of transients that some people say the only "real Alaskans" are the Eskimos and Indians. Approximately half of Alaska's population by the last census consisted of Eskimos, Indians, and Aleuts. It is quite true that these "natives," as they are commonly called in Alaska, are more closely bound to the region than the white population.

Here again the vastness of the Territory must be recalled. Even in Fairbanks, just south of the Arctic Circle, an Eskimo is rarely seen. They live still farther north in scattered villages along the flat beaches of the Arctic Coast. Hunting seal and walrus and herding reindeer along the tundra, these skillful fur-clad Americans have kept very much to their own economy for many generations and represent the only stable population in the American Arctic.

The Alaskan Indians, by contrast, are widely scattered throughout the Territory. Many make their living by trapping in the vast Interior region, selling their fur through the small trading posts along the rivers. Some $2,000,000 worth of mink, fox, beaver, marten, and muskrat is sent out to the States each year for dressing and dyeing; and while this amount is negligible as compared with the salmon and gold output, it represents an important stabilizing factor in the Alaskan economy. It is estimated that nearly half the native population, including some Eskimos along with the Indians, shoot their own meat and depend on their take of pelts, in whole or in part, as a means of livelihood. (Several thousand white men also spend their winters following long trap lines across the snow.)

Many of the Indians exist by fishing, living in small coastal settlements and in deplorable slums adjacent to the Alaskan port towns. A recent survey of the native village at Sitka showed an annual average income (including relief) of $840 per house, or $129 per person, an appallingly low sum in view of Alaska's high living costs.

Indians and Eskimos, being the original Alaskans, have hardly prospered as the result of the arrival of white men in the region. By the last census only 41 per cent of Alaska's natives were reported as employed, as compared with 62 per cent for the whites. Their tuberculosis death rate is twelve times as high as that of the Indians in the States. The Eskimos, having kept to their own economy, have suffered less. According to Froelich Rainey, Professor of Anthropology at the University of Alaska, "the Indians, apparently lacking the ability to readjust themselves and their culture to modern conditions, are rapidly disappearing; while the Eskimos, at least in several areas, have made a fairly successful adjustment and maintain themselves in native commodities with self-respect and self-assurance."

However, Professor Rainey also points out that the Eskimos' well-being is only relative; and over the years the Eskimo population, too, has declined—in sad contrast to the rapid increase of the Eskimo population in Greenland. While recent years have seen a hopeful change in the trend, it is conservatively estimated that the native population has dropped to less than half of its size at the time the Russian explorers arrived in Alaska two hundred years ago.

These are dismal facts; and if you consider the Territory's history in broad outline, it seems as dreary as the proverbial iceberg. Alaska has long been called "our Last Frontier"—but it is taking so long to develop that it looks like a dead-end street.

More than half a century ago, the historian Hubert Bancroft asked:

What land is this of which to write a history? . . . Can a country without a people furnish material for a history? . . . Few except savages have ever made their abiding-place in the wintry solitudes of Alaska; few vessels save bidarkas have ever threaded her myriad isles; few scientists have studied her geology or catalogued her fauna and flora; few surveyors have measured her snow-turbaned hills; few miners have dug for coal or iron, or prospected her mountains and streams for precious metals . . . Of settlements, there are scarce a dozen worthy of the name . . . Of the Interior, little is known.

There has been considerable progress since Mr. Bancroft penned his gloomy comments, but viewing Alaska in broad historical perspective, his description still seems sadly ap*

Considered against the backdrop of its vast potentialities, Alaska is still a land undeveloped, and it is still a "country without a people." To future historians this will probably seem the most important single fact about the rule of the Territory up to 1942.

Yet it tells you nothing about the life and work of the small group of Americans who do live in Alaska today. While it is important to view the Alaskans through a telescope, against the backdrop of history, it is also important to view them through a microscope, to find out what kind of people live in Alaska now. Although the population is still tiny, it has increased over 22 per cent in the last decade—faster than all but two of the States. While there are not many people, some of them, as much as individuals can, have made genuine contributions toward the building of Alaska.

VIII

FRONTIER RADIO

THE MIDNIGHT SUN BROADCASTING COMPANY operating just south of the Arctic Circle at Fairbanks is on the air thirteen hours a day. A thoroughly Alaskan enterprise, it was financed by the Territory's leading entrepreneur, Austin E. Lathrop, who got his nickname "Cap" when he headed north over forty-five years ago as the skipper of a small schooner. He has made several million dollars since, and has plowed much of it back into the Territory's towns. Thus he contrasts markedly with the men who have made money in Alaska only to take it Outside.

The radio transmitter station, a clean-cut white concrete building, stands by itself several miles beyond the town. Long before you reach it, you see the lonely three hundred foot antennae towering up above the rolling valley. There is an overpowering sense of space and distance in this country. Fairbanks is the last large town on the American continent, and the land to the north lies off for hundreds of miles in a vast, untracked wilderness almost completely barren of human life.

The two young engineers who operate the station also eat and sleep there, with eleven and a half miles of copper wire in the ground beneath them and with antennae high over their heads. They call it their electrical igloo. Here on the edge of the Arctic the engineers live like penthouse dwellers in New York, looking out through windows hung with Venetian blinds, sleeping on Beautyrest mattresses in a bedroom decorated with Philippine mahogany, bathing in a green-and-yellow tiled shower, and cooking their meals (and snacks for the visitors) in a gleaming kitchen that looks like the latest in *Good Housekeeping*. When the war is over Cap plans to put in six holes of golf on the neat, grassy lawn outside the building.

"Nothing," Cap says, "is too good for Alaska."

His station broadcasts as KFAR, meaning, "Key for Alaska's Riches." It is one of the signs of a new Alaska, the Alaska which is only beginning to emerge as a land of homes and culture instead of a camp for rough and tumble transients.

When KFAR signed on the air on October 1, 1939, the moment was more historic than the small crowd of Fairbanks citizens may have realized. The station's slogan, "From the Top of the World to You," has a profound implication, but it should be turned the other way. Its chief function today is bringing news to Alaskans from Outside.

Fairbanks, along with much of the Interior region, is a "dead" area for radio reception; and, since no line connection exists for teletype, KFAR gets its news mostly by short wave over two seven-wave-length rhombics, beamed for San Francisco and New York. It picks up United Press and Transradio news this way, adding to it Associated Press reports which come in by radio telegraph through the Army Signal Corps.

Like Pan American's regularly scheduled flights from Seattle to Alaska, inaugurated shortly afterward, the opening of Cap's station was an important step in joining Alaska more closely with the rest of the Union. The aerial distance was spanned by these two events as it had never been spanned before. The government's subsequent war program, providing for new air fields and an overland connection with the Territory, is so rapidly linking Alaska with the States that many people have forgotten the advance represented by these two commercial ventures, one of them financed within Alaska itself.

In the last war many trappers, mushing along their lines through the remote Interior country with sleds and Malemutes, were ignorant of the hostilities for months after they had begun. In this war many heard the KFAR announcement over their small battery sets almost as soon as it was heard by people in Chicago and New York.

It was a clear, bright day up at Fairbanks on December 7, with the sun shining on the deep snow and the temperature thirty-four below. The KFAR engineers had gone to bed early the night before, and one of them happened to wake up that morning at about eight-thirty, which was seven o'clock Hawaii time, less than an hour before the beginning of the Pearl Harbor attack. Although the station was not scheduled to go on the air till two that afternoon, Assistant Engineer August Hiebert got dressed, wandered into the control room, and idly turned on the short-wave receiver to see what he could pick up. "Just listening to the radio at that particular time," he says, "was unusual. Dozens of other Sundays the news wouldn't have been heard."

To continue his account:

Shortwave seemed to be coming in quite well, so after spinning around to see what the international stations were doing, I parked the receiver on a station which was carrying a drama.

That was about 9:10 A.M. About 9:27 or so, the drama was suddenly interrupted and an announcer said, "Japanese planes are bombing Honolulu, have attacked Pearl Harbor, and are bombing Hickam Field." I galloped into the bedroom where Stan was putting the finishing touches on getting up and shouted, "The Japs are attacking Hawaii!"

The next few minutes, as described by Chief Engineer Stanton Bennett, were full of action:

Augie called me from the control room and then swung the receiver dial over to other international stations for a confirmation of the report. I only remember saying, "They must be crazy," and turned on the shortwave transmitter filaments for a test schedule with New York. A few minutes later a second broadcast was picked up from WBOS at Boston. There now seemed little doubt of the authenticity of the reports, and the full realization came that this was war.

I contacted the radio operator at W2XYM via shortwave telephone at New York a few minutes after our 9:30 A.M. schedule. He had not yet heard any reports, then 2:30 P.M. New York time. The conversation was brief. Our remaining schedules were cancelled for the day with the comment that we had just picked up "some hot news" and the suggestion to the New York operator that he turn on his broadcast radio receiver.

The dots and dashes of our hourly press reports had already started spelling out flashes and bulletins. The local Army authorities were notified immediately by telephone of the first meager details of the raid. They in turn telephoned Anchorage, and notified the Alaska Defense Command.

The engineers had no time to eat that Sunday. They were at their posts hour after hour all day, with half empty coffee cups at their elbows as they monitored all possible stations and tapped out the reports. KFAR was on the air till after midnight, acting as the headquarters through which the community was organized for possible attack.

By 2 P.M. our press reports and official releases from Washington were quite complete. Colonel D. V. Gaffney, Commanding Officer of Ladd Field, and a few staff officers along with soldier guards arrived at the station shortly after 1:30. After carefully examining our reports, they issued several written orders for broadcast over KFAR.

A number of network releases from both CBS and NBC had been transcribed throughout the morning, and these were now released to the Alaskan listeners. Captain Harry J. Kelling, Adjutant to Colonel Gaffney, took the microphone to issue further orders to civilian workers at the air base. Civilian defense authorities placed calls through KFAR for volunteers, and announced meeting places of previously organized guards and Red Cross units. By nightfall the entire city was on a "war footing" with soldier and civilian guards on duty at key power and communication facilities, flood lights installed in some instances, and emergency squads on the alert with full instructions.

The staff of KFAR also rose ably to its responsibilities of furnishing the Alaskans with news of the war. The station made eleven short-wave connections with the States that afternoon and evening, and rebroadcast news commentators from Washington, D. C., New York, and Hollywood, as well as press bulletins. In the next few days the Alaskans heard rebroadcasts of the Churchill and Roosevelt speeches and an account direct from Manila describing the smoke pouring up from Nichols Field and the planes roaring overhead as that city was bombed. KFAR also picked up occasional short-wave broadcasts from Japan, but according to Engineer Bennett, "We only tune in on them when in need of a laugh, and when our receiving antennae are not busy on more important receptions." The station did not rebroadcast these Jap reports, for the same reason that it discontinued the practice of interrupting its programs with frequent flash bulletins. The Alaskan public, the staff felt, needed calming, not exciting. Thus America's top-of-the-world station operated with a sense of responsibility too often lacking in journalism in the States.

"Stan" and "Augie," as the two engineers are nicknamed, are only twenty-five years old. Stan got his engineering training in Oregon, before he headed north to organize KFAR.

Augie obtained his first amateur license at the age of fifteen and studied at a trade school in Los Angeles. The two Alaskans are just ordinary American boys who like to ski in wintertime at nearby Birch Hill, and play tennis in summer. Sometimes when the station is off the air, ping-pong balls can be heard clicking back and forth in the game room which Cap installed in a two-car garage built into the transmitter building. Chipping in with their friends, they sometimes charter a plane and fly off to catch the fish that fill the wild lakes, and to hunt the game so abundant in Alaska's unexplored mountains. They like to hunt with cameras as well as guns, and never tire of taking shots of the spectacular country around them

War regulations now forbid visitors; but in normal times a great many cars pull up to the station, especially on Sundays, and the guest book contains names from every State in the Union and from most foreign countries. The Alaskans themselves return again and again for a proud inspection of the modern RCA equipment. Among the most frequent visitors are groups of pretty coeds from the University of Alaska, only a mile away, who wander over the hill in their ski-suits. Augie and Stan are also popular with the women in Fairbanks, who have named them the "starvation twins" and keep them well supplied with homemade cakes and pies. However, as Stan puts it, "We are not looking for a cook— at least, we think we are too busy." Today they are even busier than usual, teaching code classes to civilian defense volunteers in the local high school; and Augie is Aircraft Warning Coordinator for the Fairbanks region.

Newcomers to Alaska are surprised by KFAR's professional touch. Like the big networks, it signs on and off the air with the sound of chimes, and maintains a continuity as smooth as most stations you hear in the States. The luxurious studio lounge, decorated with sled-dog and snowcap paintings by Alaskan artists, has Steinway and Knabe concert grand pianos. Some of the staff members on visiting radio stations Outside have been disappointed, and delighted at the same time, to find them so inferior to their own up in Alaska's "frozen waste."

It was Miriam Dickey, Cap's efficient young assistant, who first thought of the station. A Montana girl, she studied journalism at the University of Washington before she went up to Alaska. After she had persuaded Cap to build the station, he told her: "It's your problem. Do what you can with it." As secretary and treasurer of the company she still has an active hand in its operation, but the staff has expanded to a dozen people and KFAR is run on an informal teamwork basis, with the whole group, including the engineers, meeting every week to discuss technical problems and new programs

KFAR offers eight daily newscasts, interspersed with canned symphony and swing. (The Alaskans, KFAR reports, prefer symphony.) A miniature version of the major networks, it offers its own "Information, Please" program—"On the Spot"; its own "Quiz Kids'" program—"Young Alaska Speaks."

The station claims that its programs are "the most appreciated in America." While its primary coverage is the Fairbanks trading area and the railroad belt, it is also heard in outlying districts like Circle, the Kuskokwim, the Seward Peninsula, and parts of Yukon Territory; and sometimes as far north as Point Barrow and as far out to the westward as the tip of the Aleutians. Thousands of fan letters have been received from the most remote regions of Alaska.

KFAR has become an essential part of the people's lives. Prospectors and trappers and traders living in the wilderness consider their small portable radios as necessary as their guns, and watch their battery replacements as carefully as their stores of food. Natives as well as whites tune in on the station. On one occasion, when KFAR went off the air on Army orders, the frightened Indians at Fort Yukon thought the Japs had taken Alaska for sure. A few years ago the studio staff received a visit from an Indian who had come by plane all the way from the remote town of Aklavik in the Mackenzie River region of Canada. He told them he wanted to find out whether KFAR was a fake. The people in his town, he said, were quarreling about the station. Some claimed that it was real; others argued that it could not be, since its weather reports so often contradicted conditions in their town.

The radio station is reaching the Eskimos, too. For a while the KFAR staff were puzzled by persistent requests from one Eskimo settlement for a particular piece of music. Scrawled letters came into the station by the dozens, along with frequent complaints that the piece was not being played often enough. The entire staff got thoroughly tired of it, and not till a government nurse came through Fairbanks on her way Out, did they learn the reason for the demand. The Eskimos, she said, are very musically inclined. They had fashioned themselves a set of wood, skin, and sinew instruments, were organizing an orchestra, and were trying to memorize the piece by ear as they heard it over the air. Similar demands came from time to time from other Eskimo towns.

KFAR has many popular programs, but none so popular as the sportscasts in which Bud Foster, the station's youthful manager, presents a play-by-play account of the World Series and the leading football games in the States.

Since Fairbanks is a "dead" radio area, these broadcasts entail some fast and ingenious work. The only way Bud Foster can receive a play-by-play account is by radio telegraph. Working with these typed bulletins, he gets the game to the

Alaskans within a half an hour after it is actually played, banging a studio ball-and-bat device and running off victrola records of cheering and college songs for background. The result is so vivid that it's hard to believe that he isn't witnessing the game himself. It is hard work, but well worth it. Alaskans are extremely sports-minded; and if you go into the Nordale Hotel lobby when Bud's sportscasts are on, you will find the air thick with smoke, and a crowd lounging in the chromium-plated chairs and listening to the game as if their lives depended on the outcome. When the World Series is on, business almost folds up everywhere in Fairbanks, and as you walk down the street Bud's voice is heard barking over the radios of nearly all the stores in town. Bud also broadcasts local basketball, baseball, hockey, bowling, and curling matches when he is not playing in them himself.

Perhaps the most surprising thing about Cap Lathrop's radio station is the extent to which it imitates those in the States. Its whole function seems to be to transmit culture from Outside. "How about Alaskan culture?" you ask. The fact of the matter is that there is no uniquely Alaskan culture in the Territory's towns. The men and women who live there are, after all, nothing but restless Americans who were not content when the frontier was pushed to California and Washington. Most of these white people in Alaska were born and raised in the States. Even those who consider themselves residents of Alaska return to the States on frequent trips. They deeply resent any insinuation that they are different from the people back home. Because of their isolation, they are especially avid movie-goers and radio fans, and their small towns, crowded with automobiles and shops, bustle with the culture of Main Street.

IX

NEW ALASKANS

THERE ARE NOT MANY people living in Alaska; but those who do live there are proud of it. They are very much irked by the persistent concept of Alaska as a frozen waste. A few years ago the Anchorage *Times* became so annoyed that it published a magazine as "an attack on the widespread misconception that Alaska is a land of eternal ice and snow."

In its "salutation," the magazine declared:

For many years Alaskans have waged a constant battle to overcome this belief . . . In behalf of all Alaskans, we admonish outsiders that we want no sympathy because we are living on America's last frontier. We of the Northland consider it a privilege to be here. Most of us have traveled more than two thousand miles to get here and we remain because we want to—something many thousands of persons in cities in the States cannot declare truthfully.

The people who have gone to Alaska from the States are Americans—but they are Alaskans, too; and when they go back to the States on trips, they spend much of their time telling their friends and families about Alaska, showing them snapshots of the giant snowcaps and glaciers, of the big salmon, bear and moose. "It's a wonderful country," they say. "Greatest country in the world. You ought to come up."

The well-to-do Alaskans like to shop in the States. They enjoy the theater and in peacetime they enjoy speeding fast along our highways. But pretty soon they get restless; they are in a fearful rush to get back, and they wire Seattle for plane or boat reservations. As their planes take off from Boeing Field, as their ships pull out of Elliott Bay and head north, they begin to breathe more freely. They have a sense of elation, almost relief—they are so glad to leave the States behind them, so glad to be going back to Alaska.

Once Alaska "gets" you, the saying goes, you are sure to return. Enthusiasm for the country runs so strong that it nearly amounts to a cult. Many Alaskans had no intention of staying there when they first went up. For example, one of Alaska's favorite characters is sleek, dark-haired Mary Joyce, who went north in 1928, traveling as a nurse aboard a wealthy invalid's yacht. Today she operates a cedar-paneled lodge at Taku, and has crossed hundreds of miles of rough Alaskan country all by herself with a dog team. She is only one of many who became Alaskans quite by chance.

The local papers are full of stories about Alaskans going Outside and coming back. Characteristically, a paper remarked of a local merchant: "At one time he went to the States, intending to operate a chicken ranch, but the lure of Alaska was too strong and he came back." Alaskans are not in the least surprised that many of the soldiers plan to stay in the northland after the war is over.

Alaska is changing so fast that generalizations are sure to be misleading. Old and new are jumbled together. Transportation tells the story—the contrast between short, bumpy roads and speedy, far-ranging planes. The towns are a mixture of rough frontier and streamlined metropolitanism. Not so long ago Fairbanks was the "biggest log-cabin town in the world." Hundreds of cabins still stand, but as your plane circles over the town you see modern, concrete buildings, too, and a large colonial house belonging to Roy Earling (United States Smelting manager); and many small frame homes.

Only recently were the Fairbanks streets paved. The water comes out of faucets a rusty brown, so the people buy their drinking water in bottles. The Chamber of Commerce lunches at the Model Café with cans of condensed milk on the tables. But if Mrs. Cecil Robe, wife of a University of Alaska history professor, invites you to luncheon, you will find that she lives in a white Cape Cod house and serves a fancy and delicious meal. Afterwards she may ask you to play bridge with some of her friends. The ladies of Fairbanks (faculty, gold company, and Army wives) entertain frequently, especially in winter-time after the mining crowd goes Out. They prefer winter to summer "because it's more festive." Formal dress is customary at Fairbanks dinner parties, and in winter the women wear fur-lined parkas over their evening gowns and protect their slippers with reindeer-skin mukluks as they make their way from house to house through the snow.

Poverty and prosperity are jumbled in Alaska, too. The Indian shack villages on the edges of many of the towns are among the worst slums in America. But the towns have theaters and shops to rival those of large cities back home, and many Alaskans live in comfortable houses with electric refrigerators and ranges and Venetian blinds. While Cap's radio station is the most streamlined in Alaska, other towns, too, have their own stations; Juneau's KINY was the first to broadcast over national hookups from Alaska, and Anchorage's KFQD, "The Voice of the Golden North," has been operating nearly three times as long as KFAR.

Even the smallest towns have telephone systems, and a great many of them also have their own newspapers—the Nome *Nugget*, the Cordova *Times*, the Sitka *Sentinel*,

the Valdez *Miner*. Sipping cocktails in the soft light of the
Sky Lounge bar at Fairbanks, or dancing in the colorfully
decorated Bubble Room of Juneau's Baranof Hotel, you
remember with surprise that you are in Alaska. The Bubble
Room's murals were done by Alaska's Eustace Ziegler, whose
paintings of snowcap, dog, and trapper hang on the living-
room walls of well-to-do Alaskans, along with those of Ted
Lambert and the late Sidney Laurence, of whom they are
especially proud. Laurence, who studied art in New York,
Paris and Rome, spent twenty years in Alaska as a railroad-
worker, prospector and gold-miner before he began to paint
its scenery: today one of his oils of Mt. McKinley hangs in
the National Art Gallery in Washington.

The Alaskans have their own tennis, golf, and garden clubs.
Fairbanks alone has three little-theater groups, and four baseball teams in the Midnight Sun League.

The Anchorage *Times* explains:

It is no wonder that a small Alaska city of three thousand souls
should have the stores, recreational facilities, and many cultural
activities of a metropolitan city in the States . . . Most of them
came from widely scattered points in the United States . . .
Alaskans are a select group, virtually every one of them is well
traveled compared with most residents in the States.

It is hard to generalize about these people. Most of them
are individualists. Many of them, especially the oldtimers, do
not want to see Alaska develop. Others do. What most of
them have in common is an extraordinarily strong enthusiasm
for Alaska as a place to work and live. They like to see the
vast wilderness so close outside their towns. They like the
mobility of the planes. They enjoy the fact that they all know
one another—as the plane flies, gossip spreads through the
Territory as fast as through a country village. They are all

busy doing things—but not *too* busy. They take time for hunting and fishing and sport; "an Alaskan will never do today what he can do tomorrow." They are sharp in their judgments of people, and while the well-to-do Alaskans are snobbish in some ways, they are suspicious of big titles and big money, and of every sort of sham. (Movie stars like to go to Alaska because they are left alone.) "The Alaskans," another saying goes, "don't consider a man as a descendant. They consider him as an ancestor." Because of the freedom, the informality, and, above all, the easy-going *action* of life in Alaska, these people much prefer it to the States.

But how do they make their living? it is often asked. Most of them, of course, live off the gold and salmon industries—directly as workers, or indirectly as merchants. In normal times the largest year-round payroll is that of the Alaska Juneau lode mine, which employs nearly a thousand workers. Second biggest year-round payroll is that of the Alaska Railroad. The casual visitor passing through the Territory in summer may come away with the impression that all Alaskans are as highly paid as the seasonal workers. But some Alaska Railroad employees—for example, the section hands—are very low-paid, and their living conditions have long been notoriously bad; as have the conditions of workers for the Alaska Road Commission. Here again it is evident that glib generalizations about the population in Alaska are bound to be misleading.

As on any frontier, local capital is scarce. In Alaska the local businessman is apt to have his fingers in several pies at once. Maybe he has a part interest in a fish trap, or a small gold mine, but he also makes money from a hotel or a laundry or a saloon, and he may have the agency for a soap or a whiskey back in the States. Absentee ownership is the prevailing motif of the economy, and the Alaskan businessmen are typically small-town merchants, making their living from the service trades.

The small airlines, which are mostly Alaskan-owned as well as Alaskan-operated, are the outstanding local industry. Many, operating on credit, have got into financial difficulties; but it is not too much to say that they represent the leading pioneer enterprise of Alaska today. Pilots like Joe Crosson and Noel Wien, Frank Pollack, Al Monsen, Bob Reeve, Bill Lavery, Herman Lerdahl, Haakon Christensen, and Harold Gillam, are easily the most popular group in Alaska. They are popular with good reason; for they are indispensable to the region's economic and social life. There are fifty commercial planes operating out of Fairbanks alone, and every morning Cap's radio station presents a broadcast of plane movements outlining the pilots' plans for the day. For example:

Wien Alaska Airlines reports that Pilot Noel Wien today will make a trip to the upper Chandalar region with stop being made at Myrtle Creek at 10:00 A.M., where freight will be delivered for Johnny Repo's camp. Wien will continue on from there to Wiseman, and it is requested that a dog team with a large sled meet the plane upon arrival at the field to remove Suzy John, injured native woman, who this morning was discharged from the hospital. Wien is expected to return this evening to Fairbanks.

At the end of the day another broadcast tells which pilots came back, where the others are headed, how their projects panned out.

About the same number of planes operate out of Anchorage where an "On the Skyways" column published by the local weekly is read as avidly as any society page in the States.

Pilot Dan Victor went "caboose hop" to Folger to pick up Mr. and Mrs. Harold Strandberg and son, and Mr. and Mrs. Odin Strandberg and baby and return them to Anchorage for the winter . . . Pilot Haakon Christiansen made two round trips to Seward with mining men from Platinum headed Outside for the winter. The foregoing constitutes the "Flying Dane's" log for the week. He nursed a bad cold for several days and after that attended the annual meeting of the Anchorage Duck, Moose and Bicycle Society of which he is a charter member. He was named chairman of the publicity committee and a member of the refreshments committee . . .

Pilot Johnny Moore left Nome for Anchorage, but ice on the wings of his ship forced him down at Moses Point in mid-afternoon with a full load of passengers, including Everett Jones, Wilson Scott and Grant Nelson who were headed Outside to sign up with the Navy . . .

Pilot Petersen made a shakedown flight on Tuesday to see how things looked upstairs, didn't like the outlook, and returned to Anchorage. The weather cleared on Tuesday and he took off for Bethel with a load of freight and Phyllis Jones, nurse from Springfield, Illinois, headed for duty at the Government Hospital at Bethel . . .

From Seldovia, Pilot Dan Victor went to Kodiak with a consignment of vaccine from Seattle for the U.S. Naval Station at that place. Dirty weather kept Pilot Victor grounded at Kodiak for two days . . .

Henry Paneilgo was a passenger with Pilot John Walatka from the Bay to Anchorage. He is a full-blooded Eskimo, born at Barrow, and has the further distinction of being No. 1 draftee of the Bristol Bay District . . .

Clyde D. ("Doc") Gordon, head of the firm of Gordon and Company and of the Tanana Valley Truckers' Association, is flying 40 tons of supplies to Tanacross for the Office of Indian Affairs. Half of the freight is at Big Delta and the rest at a point some 35 miles above Big Delta Crossing where his new 60-foot stern-wheeler was stranded for the season when it hit a bar and was forced to tie up for the winter. Wien Airlines is doing the freighting.

Altogether, there are thirty airlines operating in Alaska, and in 1941 they carried 41,703 passengers 7,900,000 miles, and hauled 4,900,000 tons of freight. Their freight tonnage has more than tripled in six years. While Pan American is absentee-owned, most of the others are Alaskan. Many began as one-man shows; and in general, the Alaskans, financially as well as technically, have pioneered the aviation of the American Far North.

The airlines are not the only example of local capital. There are a few others. The platinum mines at Goodnews Bay, managed by the smart young Olson brothers, are by far the largest producers of that metal under the American flag. Some Alaskans own gold mines (few of them very large), some operate coal mines under lease from the federal government, and some have small sawmills and cold-storage plants. Others have developed small fur farms and fisheries—notably Earl Ohmer, "shrimp king," of Petersburg.

Earl Ohmer is one of the outstanding Alaskans and also one of the most colorful. As the boat pulls into Petersburg, the bearded man is likely to be standing on the dock wearing a cowboy hat and fancy western regalia, with a gold nugget dangling from his watch-chain. His office near by is a small dark hole smelling of fish and crowded with elkhorns, pictures of rearing horses, mink skins, guns, and totem poles. Over his desk is a huge eagle which he shot himself. Ohmer left the Oregon cow range in 1916 ("too many barb-wire fences, they were crowding out the free rangers"), and the same year started the first shrimp business in Alaska, using a small boat which he built himself. Today his annual sales are over $350,000—including salmon, shrimp, and other fish, as well as mink, which he raises on a farm near by. He is chairman of the Alaska Game Commission, a board of resident Alaskans which advises the federal government on game regulation.

The leading Alaskan businessman, however, is Cap Lathrop. Cap is remarkable in that he represents some of the spirit of both old and new Alaska. Like many other sourdoughs, he worked doggedly in the early days in a rough country under primitive conditions. But while others took their money Outside, he stayed to build his radio station, theaters, and other properties in a modern Alaska which is just beginning to develop into a land of homes instead of a land of transients—a land where the modern and the streamlined are sought after, in all aspects of life and culture.

To see Cap walking rapidly down the Fairbanks street in his usual preoccupied manner, you would never know that he is a millionaire. Casually dressed, with a battered old hat set back on his head, the rugged white-headed man looks more like the local carpenter. He lives simply, sharing some rooms in his apartment house with the man who runs the reels in his corner theater. (He used to have an apartment for himself, but gave it up to one of his newscasters who got married and needed a place to live.) He eats most of his meals at the counters of the Co-op Drugstore, the Model Café, and the Pioneer Grill.

Cap dislikes it when anyone calls him an oldtimer. "Oldtimer," he says. "All this oldtime-Alaska stuff. Why not talk about something new?"

Cap is seventy-seven, but still so energetic and industrious that he looks no more than sixty. Born in Lapeer, Michigan, he attended public schools in the Middle West. His business career began when he heard the news of the Seattle fire in 1889. Jumping the next train he arrived there before the city stopped smoking and made a lot of money razing burned structures. Later, he was known in Seattle as the "boy contractor," owning forty teams of horses at the age of twenty-four. He built a local railroad and ran the first train over its track; managed a large-scale chicken ranch; and lost his money in the '93 panic. He decided to try his luck in Alaska, borrowed money to buy part interest in a small steam schooner, and headed north. He has been an Alaskan ever since.

It is worthy of note that Alaska's leading businessman never prospected for gold or made any money in it. It is also notable that even Cap has Outside financial interests. He is a Director of the Olympia Brewing Co. of Olympia, Washington, whose agency he handles for western Alaska. But most of his money has been made from Alaskan operations. The most profitable is a coal mine. The largest in Alaska, it supplies fuel for the United States Smelting dredges and for the Army. Apart from the mine, most of his fortune has been made in transfer and theater businesses and apartment houses in the growing frontier settlements. "I've just been around the country, that's all," he says with a shrewd smile. "First one town sprung up and then another. That's the way it happened."

Cap's apartment and theater buildings in the seaport town of Cordova were built nearly twenty years ago, but they are still the best in town. He owns the only theater in Anchorage, and had started construction of a second when war broke out. He also owns the only two theaters in Fairbanks. The Empress Theater, built back in 1927, was the first concrete structure in the Interior. Sourdoughs said a concrete building couldn't stand up under the cold winters, and government officials watched it carefully for "checking" for several years before they ventured to put up the large Fairbanks Federal Building. The Lacey Street Theater, built in 1940, cost $175,000 for a five-hundred-and-fifty-chair house, and Cap thinks it is the most expensive for its size in all America. He has built a luxurious lounge on the second floor where Alaskans wait between shows in expensive leather chairs, gazing at a modernistic carpet copied from the one in the R.C.A. Building in New York.

Cap also owns the *News-Miner,* the only newspaper in Fairbanks till *Jessen's Weekly* was started in 1942, and he owns the only radio station. His apartment house, tenanted by the radio and newspaper staffs, and other professionals, is far more modern than any other in town. It has a bowling alley in the basement and a laundry on the roof.

"Why do they always put laundries down in the cellar?" Cap asks. "I think they belong on top."

Cap dislikes being called a millionaire almost as much as he dislikes being called an oldtimer. When I asked him why he invested his money in Alaska instead of the States, he began to chuckle. "Their pencil is too sharp for me Outside," he remarked. "I'm only used to handling nickels and quarters."

Cap's own pencil is plenty sharp, as anyone who has dealt with him can testify, and he has made a large part of his millions in "nickel-and-quarter" transactions. (He charges ten cents for his newspaper, sixty cents for a movie at the Lacey Street Theater.) Undoubtedly one reason for his success has been the fact that he has stuck to a cash business, in contrast with many other local enterprises which have operated on seasonal credit and had financial difficulties as a result.

Cap is a shrewd operator in late nineteenth century style, and has built and managed his interests as business propositions; but he runs the radio station as a piece of philanthropy. During the ceremonies of its opening, he was so overcome with emotion that he broke down and sobbed. "I feel privileged," he told the Fairbanks crowd that night, "to give this station to my people." All of its profits have gone into a fund for expansion. Like many another businessman, Cap combines hard-driving acquisitiveness with great personal warmth, even a streak of sentimentality.

Cap has many friends in Alaska, but he also has enemies— even at Fairbanks where his handsome white apartment house and theater building set the tone of the main street.

"Cap's a monopolist," one merchant told me, after looking uneasily around his store. "Why do you suppose he put up that second theater when he already had one? Because he wanted to keep somebody else from doing it. Can't stand competition. He's trying to do the same thing down at Anchorage. Wants to hog everything."

Others complained about prices. "He does things in a big way," they told me, "but he sure soaks you for it. You don't get anything for nothing at Cap's."

It is not surprising that animosity should arise against Cap's small northern empire. Monopoly has never been popular on our frontiers, and some people are irritated by the power of Cap's grip over the town and its press. They point out that when Governor Gruening issued a message to the people of Alaska at the close of the 1941 legislature's session, Cap's *News-Miner* failed to print it, nor was it given publicity over his radio station. It was well known that Cap, along with absentee business interests, opposed the Governor's modern tax program.

It may seem paradoxical that the "builder of Alaska," as Cap has been called—the man who has done more than any other individual to make the Territory's towns good places to live in—should oppose a program to raise taxes for Territorial needs. But the conflict has been a familiar one in America, since Roosevelt entered the White House. True to form, Cap is a Republican. He went to the States in 1928 and 1932 as National Committeeman from Alaska. While less active, he continues to be a factor in party politics in the Territory. Business is business, and taxes are taxes, even up near the Arctic Circle, and even Alaska has its own miniature business-and-government controversies.

Alaska has had its labor disputes, too. Already it has had a colorful, rough-and-tumble trade-union history. The fishing unions have been largely run from San Francisco and Seattle, like the rest of the salmon operation. In the more recent organization of the miners Alaska has developed a labor movement more its own.

If you wander across the street, you will see right behind Cap's modern apartment house a small frame shack with a stovepipe sticking up from the roof and a black-lettered sign by the door reading "C.I.O." If it is cold weather, smoke will be puffing out of the pipe, and you will find a group of miners sitting around the stove inside. Wearing high boots and flannel shirts, these men look like frontiersmen—and they are.

They are Alaskans. They live there. They work there. They are trying to make it a better place to do both. Capable, keen-minded W. A. Rasmussen, who is Acting C.I.O. Field Representative, originally came from Norway where his father was a leader in the cooperative movement; he learned his trade unionism as a boy, working in the Narvik iron mines. Today he is wholeheartedly Alaskan. He has worked in Alaska fourteen years, and has had experience in both its major industries. He was employed in the Alaska Juneau gold mine seven years; the rest of the time he trolled for salmon, watched a fish trap, and clerked in the stores. Rasmussen lives in a small frame house in Juneau, with an attractive young wife and their Alaskan-born son.

Like Cap, Rasmussen is devoted to Alaska. Like Cap, he has had some tough going there, but of a somewhat different variety. When he first arrived in Fairbanks in the spring of 1939 to organize the miners, he was kidnaped, beaten up, and run out of town, much as labor organizers have been run out of small towns in Alabama, Tennessee, and other undeveloped regions. The gang who did the job put him on a train and told him to keep going, but he got off at the first stop, telephoned the United States Marshal for protection, and took the next train back. He organized the miners, too, and their 1941 strike resulted, among other things, in improved living conditions in bunkhouses and cookhouses of the United States Smelting camps, some of which, according to the miners, were deplorable—little better than the old camps of '98.

Mr. Rasmussen and his men, according to familiar pattern, have been attacked as "radicals," but no stockholder could have been more solicitous of the mining properties than they were when they pulled that strike. The company's eight giant dredges, miles apart in the wilderness, were stopped one by one according to a previously prepared plan, in order to ease the load on the power plant. Despite the bitterness of the strike, one of the company officials later informally congratulated union leaders for the skillful caution they exercised during the course of it.

Cap and Rasmussen are no friends, but each, in his own way, has made a contribution toward the maturity of Alaska. While Cap's handsome concrete buildings are the more tangible departure from the shoulder-shrugging philosophy of transients, Mr. Rasmussen's achievements are equally real, and perhaps more important in long-range terms. He is a thoroughly unassuming man, quick to give credit to his associates; but as you talk with him you find that he has vision for Alaska that is equaled by few men in the Territory, for he thinks in terms of the ordinary men and women who work there. Their security, he maintains, is a first essential for a more stable population. Even the high seasonal wages, he points out, are not what they seem when a man has to stretch them over the whole year. An example of his achievements is the job seniority agreement that the miners' union recently gained from United States Smelting, guaranteeing the workers of one season first preference for employment in the next. Mr. Rasmussen has a keen and active interest in Territorial politics, supporting progressive legislation like Governor Gruening's modern tax program at the 1941 legislature. He is also unusually alert to Alaska's role in world affairs, and he is a strong anti-fascist—more eloquently so than anyone else I met in the Territory.

The fourth All-Alaska Labor Convention, sponsored by the C.I.O., was held in Juneau early in 1942 with delegates from Alaska locals of the Mine Workers, Longshoremen, Transport Workers, Retail Clerks, Woodworkers, Agricultural, Cannery and Packing Workers, and several others. Starting off with the reading of a telegram from Philip Murray, ALASKA IS ONE OF THE MOST IMPORTANT OUTPOSTS AND YOUR INITIATIVE FOR LABOR'S EFFECTIVE PARTICIPATION IN THE WAR TO VICTORY IS HEARTILY TO BE WELCOMED, the three-day gathering was truly Alaskan—reflecting the ever recurring uncertainty of transportation. ("Brother Scheel said he had a plan for the Fishermen's Union which was coming on the boat and he hoped it would arrive in time.") The men discussed many problems of work and life in the Territory; and went on record against excessive price raising, for a Territorial subsidy to individual prospectors, for the establishment of a tubercular sanitarium and a marine hospital, for an expanded school system and a more adequate health program for children in remote rural areas, and for measures more specifically related to conditions of work themselves.

Alaska has its business and labor leaders; it has a few farmers, too. Outstanding among them is Charlie Creamer, who came north with his wife in 1904. His 327-acre Fairbanks dairy farm is a real show place, with the big barn and farmhouse, as well as the delivery trucks, nattily painted white with black trim. When he erected the new buildings a few years ago, he gave a barn-warming dance attended by over a thousand people. Charlie Creamer works hard—and as he comes in from the fields, a huge, towering man clad in overalls and high shoes, he looks it—but he's never too tired to take you around the place, to show you his eighty-four head of Guernseys and Holsteins, and to talk about the problems of Alaska's agriculture.

There are thousands of acres in the Tanana Valley surrounding Fairbanks, he says, that are fit for farming. Crops grow well in the earth above the permanent frost. Yet nothing is commercially harvested but potatoes and "you can count the spud farmers on the fingers of one hand." He doesn't bother with vegetables himself, although he raises the hay for his cows. The trouble is not the country, he says, it is costs—and the market. He paid $20,000 to build his barn—at least twice as much as he would have had to pay in the States. "People are so educated to a tin can," he told me, "that strawberries and raspberries rot on the vine. If they could ship fresh milk in, I guess we'd have to quit that, too."

As it is, Charlie Creamer makes a lot of money from his dairy business, charging twenty-five cents a quart for his milk; and some of his customers complain in turn that he is unnecessarily boosting their cost of living.

Although there are a few individual farms, most Alaskan agriculture (what there is of it) is concentrated at the government's Matanuska Valley colony near Anchorage. Matanuska presents such a contrast with the rest of Alaska that the first sight of it is nothing short of amazing. I made the 325-mile trip down the Alaska Railroad from Fairbanks to Matanuska in one day, traveling with Colonel Otto Ohlson, the road's manager, in his speeder—a metal-wheeled DeSoto which ran along the tracks. It was a long but breath-taking journey. We left Fairbanks at seven in the morning, and hour after hour we hurtled noiselessly along through lonely tundra country, past enormous snow-covered peaks. We stopped for a brief luncheon at Curry where the railroad runs a green-painted wooden hotel, one of the only two restaurants on the lonely route. Now and then ptarmigan and spruce hens whirred in the brush, and the Colonel stopped the speeder, grabbed his gun and scrambled after them. "I wonder where that freight is," he remarked, as we resumed our trip after one of these episodes, moving faster and faster, swinging around the curves at a dizzying rate of speed. Once we nearly collided with a cow moose which lumbered off the track into the woods just in time. It was a country even more rugged than the Swiss Alps, and so lonely that it seemed much more spectacular. It seemed as if we were reaching the remotest parts of the Northland, when suddenly the Colonel turned his speeder off on a side spur; and as we flew along through the early dusk, an American farm community appeared before us, with red barns and log farmhouses neatly arranged around a water tower. It looked both peaceful and productive against the backdrop of lofty white Pioneer Peak.

The Matanuska project, I found, was not very peaceful, and it was by no means as productive as it could be. In 1935, when the Federal Emergency Relief Administration shipped two hundred families to Alaska from the drought-stricken and distressed areas in the States, no one knew quite how it would turn out. There have been many difficulties and dissensions at Matanuska—and the government has been subjected to a great deal of criticism for its management of the colony, some of which is dealt with elsewhere in this book. In view of the small output of the Matanuska farms the project most certainly cannot be called an unqualified success. But neither can it be called an unqualified failure, and in the barrage of ridicule that Matanuska has received, its accomplishments have been almost entirely obscured.

In 1941 the Matanuska Valley Farmers Cooperating Association paid farmers of the valley $105,000, 54% more than in 1940. At least half of them sold over $600 worth, nearly a dozen over $1,000 worth. This does not mean as much as it might, because the more prosperous farmers were making their money in dairying. The 400 head of high-grade Guernsey dairy cattle are Matanuska's principal profit-producers today. Yet Matanuska was also growing and marketing some vegetables; and while the output was ridiculously small compared with the possibilities, the fact that there was any at all was a revolutionary advance for Alaska and meant a great deal in terms of the future. They were producing excellent potatoes—Irish Cobblers, Early Ohio, Arctic Seedling, and Gold Coin—with yields varying from two to four hundred bushels per acre. They were producing enormous and delicious cabbage, weighing up to forty-five pounds, cauliflower, celery, parsnips, and beets, raspberries, strawberries, blueberries, and gooseberries. Over a period of years Siberian wheat at the government's nearby Experiment Station has yielded twenty-two bushels an acre; barley, twenty-six; and oats, forty-five.

Land has been cleared of spruce, birch, and cottonwood. Log houses and red barns have been built. Wells have been dug. As you bump along the roads with a Matanuska farmer in his jalopy and see these things, it looks like countryside in Wisconsin or Minnesota. There are several churches, an up-to-date high school, and a grade school at Palmer, which is the center of the Matanuska community. Even as a social experiment the project has progressed. Since the Matanuska Valley Cooperating Association was organized in the fall of 1936, the farmers have taken an increasing part in the management of their own affairs. The Association operates a creamery, a trading post, a warehouse, a hospital, a recreation center, a power plant, a lodge and a cold storage plant.

Although few people in Alaska recognize them as such, the producing farmers at Matanuska are pioneers. They have accomplished the beginning of agriculture in the Northland, and are therefore outstanding among the new Alaskans.

The newest Alaskans of all are to be found at the university in Fairbanks. It was a bright autumn afternoon when I drove out to the university, bumping along a typical dirt road, passing a farm or two with shocks of grain in the fields around the neat houses and barns. It was hard to believe that we were close to the Arctic Circle. The rolling valley was sparsely wooded with clumps of birch among the scraggly evergreens, and as we looked ahead the countryside seemed to gleam with white bark and golden leaves. It was much like New England in the fall, except that there was little color in the foliage—

only the gold of the birch which looked almost translucent under the bright blue sky.

The university consists of eight small buildings clustering under a water tower on the side of a hill. They are unpretentious—but the campus has one of the most spectacular settings in America. From their classrooms students view the distant white peaks of the Alaska Range rimming the wild valley, and on clear days they can see Mount McKinley itself, highest mountain on the continent, looking like a low-hanging cloud or a mirage.

On climbing the steps of the Ben Eielson Memorial Building, I was ushered into the president's office. The head of America's northernmost university was wearing suspenders over his red-and-blue checked lumberjack shirt, and his conversation was as vivid as his costume. A Pennsylvania farm boy, Charles Bunnell graduated from Bucknell University and migrated to Alaska in 1900 to teach at an Indian school on Wood Island near Kodiak. He taught, practiced law, and served as a federal judge in Alaska until he took charge of the university in 1922. He has been its president ever since, and lives by himself in a small frame home a short way down the hill.

Dr. Bunnell is tired and worn from the hard work he has put in trying to develop higher education in Alaska. Like many others of the Territory's leaders, he is intensely devoted to the region.

"I don't know why so many people live in the States," he told me with an ironic sigh, "that misty, musty place—the States."

The University of Alaska had six students on its first day of enrollment in 1922. In 1941 it had nearly three hundred. Started as a federal land-grant college, it is supported chiefly

by Territorial funds. Since these usually amount to less than
$150,000 a year, Dr. Bunnell has had a struggle to build a
college that would rival those back home. He works hard at
the job, getting up before six every morning, busying himself
all day and much of the evening with its administrative, classroom, and student problems. Sometimes he puts on his old
clothes and does a carpentering job. It has been a hard pull,
and he is justly proud of the fact that the university has become a member of the Northwest Association of Secondary
and Higher Schools, with its credits accepted anywhere. He
is proud that its library has over 19,000 bound volumes and
subscribes to over 130 magazines. He is proudest of all, however, of the students themselves, and they are no ordinary
students.

"Nobody's *sent* to college here," Dr. Bunnell told me.
"These boys have rustled freight and dug ditches. They know
how to work."

It is said that the University of Alaska has a larger proportion of students earning their way than any college in the
country. The college has a democratic, straightforward
atmosphere about it—which is very refreshing after the Gothic
decadence of some institutions of higher learning in the
States. A room in one of the dormitories costs ten dollars a
month; board can be had for thirty-five. There is no tuition
fee for Alaskans. Students do much of the work and wait on
table. The milk, as well as some of the fresh vegetables and
meat, is supplied from the Agricultural Experiment Station
near by. While the college offers the traditional liberal arts
courses, by far the biggest department is mining; and in
general there is emphasis on the practical rather than the
academic. In addition to its regular work, the university con-
ducts special extension courses for prospectors and miners

throughout the Territory, in which nearly four thousand men have been enrolled in the past six years.

University of Alaska students get no vacations during the school year, and when summertime comes and graduation day rolls around most of them pack up their books and go, not on vacation, but to work. Some get jobs in the towns, as they stir with the life and trade created by the Territory's seasonal industries. Many others board planes for mining districts, some flying hundreds of miles for summer jobs at remote points like Nome and Candle. "They have a hundred and twenty-one working days every summer," says Dr. Bunnell. Students who work in the gold mines make nearly enough money to carry them through the school year, and in addition their summer jobs serve as a laboratory where they can learn the practical application of their class work.

The university is a "workingman's college," but it is still a college with all the fixings. In spring and fall the students play hockey and baseball. They have their own Fight Song: "Cheer for the Polar Bears, Mighty Men Are They." In the winter they do a lot of skiing. The university has heavy co-ed romances, bitter faculty feuds, just like any other. It has its own college paper, the *Farthest-North Collegian,* and it is building its own traditions, including a ceremonial bonfire staged for the incoming Freshmen every fall.

Dr. Bunnell takes an even greater pleasure in the bonfire than his students do. As the afternoon turned into dusk, and we looked out of his window, he pointed to what looked like a giant scarecrow towering at the edge of the wilderness.

"The Freshmen have been building it all week," he told me, "and they have to stand guard; otherwise the upper-class men would come and knock it down."

As it grew darker, the students began to wander down the

hill toward the enormous bonfire, and Dr. Bunnell followed. They stood in silence to watch him set it ablaze with a burning torch. The Freshmen then crowded forward with sticks to carry the flame to small fires they had laid in a circle around it. As the roaring blaze climbed higher and higher the pole shifted as if it were about to topple. The students moved back and, standing with the light reflected in their faces, they sang their *Alma Mater.*

> All hail Alaska, sing her praise,
> Our home of carefree college days;
> A pioneer, we see thee stand
> Champion of far north frontier land.

While most of the university's students come from the Territory's towns, between a quarter and a third of them migrate up from the States for the purpose of working their way through college in Alaska. The 1939–40 student body contained representatives from twenty-five states. Although the biggest groups came from California, Washington, and Oregon, there were boys and girls from such widely separated parts as Maine, North Dakota, and Maryland. There are few Eskimo or Indian students at the University of Alaska— a startling fact, since they comprise half the population and it is the only institution of higher learning in the Territory.

If you wander into the university museum, you will see a rare combination of exhibits. The white head of an albino moose. A pair of caribou horns, locked in telephone wire. Drinking cups used on the dirigible that flew over the Pole from Spitsbergen to Teller. A Russian plaque claiming rights to Alaskan territory. Eskimo ivory carvings and hunting helmets. Spear throwers from various parts of the Arctic Coast. An automobile built in 1905 in Skagway by Sourdough Robert

Sheldon, who had never seen one. (He got his ideas from a picture of a Ford marine motor.)

"I built it to make time with a girl," says sharp-witted "Bobby" Sheldon, for many years postmaster of Fairbanks and in charge of tourist transportation in McKinley Park. "The other guy had a carriage and a team of horses. I figured I had to go him one better."

At the museum you can also see the printing press that ran off Alaska's first newspaper at Fort Adams on the Yukon in 1894.

The University of Alaska is the recognized center of scientific and historical research in the American Far North, and it has done work as exciting as it is little known. It was the headquarters of one of the international Second Polar Year expeditions in 1933, in which over thirty nations participated. It has conducted extensive archæological excavations on St. Lawrence Island under the direction of Otto Geist, tracing the development of Eskimo culture for a period of over two thousand years. In cooperation with the American Museum of Natural History the university has made further archæological studies on the Alaskan mainland and, according to Anthropology Professor Froelich Rainey, they found ivory carvings far more elaborate than any produced by the Eskimos at a lonely place called Ipiutak, and the traces of a mysterious population of three to four thousand people, with an ancient cemetery extending four and a half miles. The university has also cooperated with the American Museum in paleontological studies of the huge mastodon bones scooped up by the United States Smelting dredges from the silt and mud of thawing ground back of Fairbanks.

The University of Alaska has some distinguished young professors. It occupies a role of great importance in the life of the Territory. But because of limited funds, in some years it has had to turn away as many students as it admitted. It has no infirmary. It needs a new boiler generator. Its men's dormitory is a ramshackle affair, referred to by one leading member of the faculty as a "rats' nest." The old wooden buildings are difficult to heat. All these things President Bunnell has very much on his mind, and when he asked the 1941 legislature for $362,000 for buildings and equipment, he was speaking in terms of these needs. Yet he got only $60,000. "Let it drift," one Senator remarked.

"It is too bad," says President Bunnell. "We have the opportunity to do so much more."

There is one very fundamental thing to be appreciated about the University of Alaska. From the time of its founding through 1942 the great majority of its students have stayed to live and work in the Territory. Some of them now occupy important government posts. One is superintendent of a large United States Smelting dredge operation.

"There's still quite a halo about going Outside," Dr. Bunnell told me, "but more and more are staying in Alaska." A while ago he began sending "first" shoes and socks to the babies of University graduates. Today he's buying them by the dozen.

Sitting in the university's bleak, dingy dining room, we watched the students crowded around the tables, laughing and kidding and arguing. As the roar of their conversation rose higher and higher, after the fashion of all college dining rooms, Dr. Bunnell turned to me and remarked:

"We may get licked today in what we are trying to do; but in the long run, these younger people will be the hope. We like to talk about things; but I'm telling you—this next generation will be doing them."

When the war began, Dr. Bunnell told his students: "A rough house is asked for and a rough house it is going to be. . . . And in the meantime, and while we are being put to the test, we are going to build better."

Faculty members began all-night relay watches at the power house, and the blackouts started. "It is essential," warned the *Farthest-North Collegian*, "that every person have access to warm clothing and a flashlight. Under the present circumstances there is more danger of freezing to death than of being shot.

"Precautions have disrupted the normal way of living to a certain extent. Snowsuits and mukluks dangle in precarious and handy positions about the various rooms, and during blackout time the dormitory dates all seem to leave home. Most of the men may be found with their dates in Harriet Hess Hall's lounge."

The college initiated extensive war activity, and when spring came, the Farm Extension Department began a series of gardening classes. Almost every family in Fairbanks now has a Victory Garden.

All over the Territory, the Alaskans—new and old, whites, Eskimos and Indians—got busy with war work. Cap Lathrop turned over his mikes to the Army. Red Cross sewing machines were busy day and night in the ballroom of his Empress Theater, and he offered the basements of all his concrete buildings for bomb shelters.

When war began the Matanuska farm colony planned to increase its production from 25 to 50 per cent. ("Fill the ships with those supplies essential to the defense of Alaska. We'll give you as much foodstuff as our farms will produce.") Labor too pledged its aid in the war, and the All-Alaska Labor Convention declared its first purpose was: "To formulate a program for effective participation in the war," and passed resolutions urging payroll allotments for defense bonds and favoring peaceful settlement of labor disputes.

The Alaskans all began to get ready for trouble. They began buying Defense Bonds for a Flying Fortress to be named, "The Spirit of Alaska." From the bleak Aleutians where "Squeaky" Anderson is bossing the Y.P. boat patrol up to remote Arctic villages where Eskimos are watching the skies and guarding brand new weather stations, they all got busy. Small Eskimo communities purchased Defense Bonds, too—Savoonga on St. Lawrence Island bought $10,000 worth from its store profits. Hundreds of Eskimo women and children began sewing mukluks, parkas, fur pants, and mittens for the soldiers, selling them through the Skin Sewers Co-operative Association at Nome.

Up at remote Point Barrow, the Eskimos began holding nightly blackouts and holding twenty-four-hour guard, and according to Mrs. Howard Burkher, Indian Affairs instructor at Point Barrow, the war has defined democracy for them more than any other experience they have had "under the wing of the big Eagle in Washington." Soon after the attack on Pearl Harbor, a group of Eskimos from Point Barrow, arriving at Nome to volunteer for service in the Army, showed the boys from the States that they were "crack shots with rifles and have many times demonstrated they can hit a two-inch bull's-eye at 75 yards. They can run all day beside a dogsled. They can travel all day on snowshoes. They are skilled in the use of knives." Eskimos drafted into the Army are now serving along with the white soldiers at the major army posts in Alaska.

Alaska's pilots got busy hauling Army personnel and construction workers and war freight, and in some cases flying volunteer patrols. There is one "sourdough" pilot who stands out above all others, having made an unrivaled contribution to the war—namely, Brigadier General James H. ("Jimmy") Doolittle. Son of a Gold Rush stampeder, Doolittle spent his boyhood in Nome; and although he had spent most of his life "Outside" the Territory, when the Tokyo raid occurred Alaska claimed him as its own. The *Alaska Weekly*, carrying a "FULL LIFE STORY OF NOME-TOWN BOY MADE GOOD," related:

When the Wright brothers startled the world in 1903 with the first airplane flight at Kitty Hawk, North Carolina, there was a peewee schoolboy in Nome who immediately began folding paper planes and sailing them across the classroom. Oldtimers recall Jimmy as "the kid who built kites that would fly, and airplanes that wouldn't." Between fights in the muddy streets that were Nome, Jimmy read every word in every piece of printed matter that found its way north—not about fighters, but about fliers. It didn't take Jimmy long to learn—the hard way—that you didn't need a license to be taught at Nome. Even the "little kids" were harder than the gold their Dads grubbed for . . . today that boy won the Congressional Medal of Honor . . . and the two qualities, fighting and flying, which have distinguished his every act since childhood, were acquired in that "hell-roaring" mining camp of Nome.

With this fighting, flying example before them, the people in Alaska are impatiently looking Westward. As the Japanese attacked the Aleutians, Alaska's Secretary, Bob Bartlett, who has spent his life in the Territory and knows its people well, said:

"Alaskans have no inclination to take the attack lightly. They feel just as concerned about the invasion as the Japs would, were we to take some of their northern islands. But there has been little jitteriness in the Territory. Some people have left, of course, but most of the Alaskans have stayed, and they are holding tough. Morale is high. Should the Japs land in force on the mainland they are going to meet guerrilla fighters of the kind the Germans have encountered in Russia. Alaska miners and Alaska fishermen are ready to get in there and pitch. They aren't going to surrender. They're going to fight. And sensible as they are of the fact that the United States must furnish arms all over the world, Alaskans feel the war would be shortened a lot if we could move to kick the Japs out of the Aleutians and do the invading ourselves from now on."

X

PRIDE AND POLITICS

THE ALASKAN political temper is very difficult to understand. It is almost as contradictory as the region's hot-and-cold weather, almost as tricky as the inverted temperatures and the erratic compass deviations that plague its airplane pilots. A study of it is complicated by high-running pride and prejudice in the Territory and by the Alaskans' fondness for telling tall stories. One of the first things a reporter learns there is to disbelieve a large part of what he is told. Isolated in their frontier towns the Alaskans always like to gossip. Among themselves, the oldtimers enjoy a story with a "kick" to it and for the outsiders they will make it one better. They like to bedevil tourists with fictitious tales of long spaghetti-like ice-worms that live in the glaciers. While not unfriendly, they regard reporters, too, with a sly humor. It is hard to tell whether they enjoy being investigated, or whether they resent it.

A reporter arriving in Alaska is alarmed at first at the bitterness that appears to exist toward American long-range administration. Since war started, that kind of talk has simmered down, but in normal times, as loquacious old sourdoughs lean against the small-town bars and counters, the air seems to buzz with complaints. Alaska, they tell you, is being red-taped to death by "bureaucrats," plagued by junketing carpet-baggers, run by remote control from a point thousands of miles away; the residents themselves have no say, and government under the President is as bad as it used to be under the Czar. From statements like these a newcomer gets the first impression that our government of the Territory has been tyrannical, that "home rule" is the burning political issue of the region and that civilian morale is dangerously low.

The first impression, however, is largely mistaken on all three counts. The Alaskans are passionately patriotic when it comes to a showdown. In the last World War they contributed a greater proportion of their population than any State. In this war, too, they are doing more than their share: in May, 1942, they oversubscribed their war bond quota by nearly 300 per cent, surpassing every State in the Union. Although the Alaskans, especially the oldtimers, bear a certain amount of resentment toward the "bureaucrats in Washington," it does not run deep. The feeling is more one of irritation and hurt than of bitterness. To the extent that they are resentful, it is not because they have been crushed under the heel of tyranny, but because they have been ignored and pushed around. Home rule is not the basic issue in the political life of the Territory, nor does resentment exist against the government as a whole. The picture is complex: while the work of some government departments is much disliked, the performance of others is equally appreciated.

The first thing that strikes you about the government structure of Alaska is the dominant function of the federal government. If you go into the Federal Building at Juneau, on a hillside above the jumble of steep streets and roofs, you begin to see what the Alaskans mean when they talk about "bureaucracy." As you look up to the lobby Directory, you see their titles inscribed in a long list—the Office of

Indian Affairs, the Game Commission, the Post Office, the Customs, and many others; and you can hear the high-pitched chirp of the Army Signal Corps wireless which handles all telegraphic communications with the States. Day and night the incessant shrill sound continues, keeping Alaska in touch with the "Outside." There are over fifty federal agencies operating in Alaska, so crowded together that it seems as if there were even more. In normal times it is estimated that one out of every five workers in Alaska is employed either full or part time by the federal government. The federal government owns over 98 per cent of all the land and most of the resources.

Throughout Alaska, imposing concrete federal buildings stand high above the wooden roofs of the frontier towns around them. A few blocks down the hill from Juneau's Federal Building the small, unpretentious Territorial Building stands in symbolic contrast. While the federal government normally spends from $12,000,000 to $15,000,000 a year in Alaska, the Territory spends approximately $2,000,000. Most of this goes for roads and schools (Alaska supports the educational system for its white population), for the university, the Pioneers Home, old age pensions, aid to aviation and mining. The Alaskan legislature—a sixteen-man House and an eight-man Senate—meets every other year at United States Government expense for a sixty-day session in the Federal Building. Its powers are limited by Act of Congress and its actions are subject to the veto of the Governor, who cannot be overridden except by a two-thirds vote of both Houses. The Governor and the Secretary of Alaska are federal officials appointed by the President of the United States, although the Territory has the right to elect certain other officials, among them an Attorney General, an Auditor, a Treasurer, and a Highway Engineer.

The Alaskans' resentment, such as it is, is not so strong in coastal towns like Juneau as in the inland towns of Anchorage and Fairbanks, where, as one federal official admitted, there exists a "real ingrained feeling of hurt and wrong." When asked what harm they have suffered at the hands of "bureaucrats," the Alaskans, almost without exception, name the Department of the Interior and its Secretary, Harold Ickes.

A mere mention of the Secretary's name in Alaska is apt to produce outbursts of annoyance and wrath. At its last session the legislature passed a memorial urging the President to accept his resignation, declaring in part:

WHEREAS the Honorable Secretary seeks to nullify democratic procedure in force in Alaska . . .

WHEREAS his attitude toward matters arising concerning the Territory is so consistently in opposition to the attitude of the great majority of the citizens of the Territory . . . and they believe his continuance in office as Secretary of the Interior will retard industry and settlement, and do great general harm within the Territory;

Now THEREFORE WE, the Alaska Legislature in Fifteenth Regular Session, respectfully pray that the resignation of the Honorable Harold L. Ickes from the Secretaryship of the Department of the Interior be immediately accepted and a successor be appointed who will have a sympathetic understanding viewpoint toward Alaska, its problems and its future, and if such resignation be not accepted, that then all control now belonging to the Secretary of the Interior respecting the Territory of Alaska be transferred to the Secretary of Commerce or the Secretary of Agriculture.

The Department of the Interior plays a powerful role in the government of Alaska. It controls all the land, except the strip along the southeastern coast which comes under the Department of Agriculture; many of the most important agencies operating in the Territory come under its wing; and the Governor of Alaska makes his annual report not to the President who appointed him, but to Secretary Ickes. Curiously, the emblem on the Governor's report is not the Territorial dipper and stars but the sketch of buffalo and plains which decorates official Interior Department publications in the States. More important, the Interior Department title is lettered on the shabby cars of the much-hated Alaska Railroad, which it also operates. Aside from the one in Panama, the Alaska Railroad is the only railroad of any length that is owned by the federal government. As its slow-moving trains chug, creak, and rattle over steep divides, along the edges of canyons, past glaciers and snowcaps, the road is rough in more ways than one—Ickes himself once remarked that you have to be an acrobat to ride on it. The railroad is the main artery of the economic life of inland Alaska, and also the main artery of Alaskan political resentment. It is not surprising that ill-feeling against the "bureaucrats" has been strongest in the towns along its track, for in recent years the line has been run in flagrant disregard of the people who have to use it.

Congress originally decided to build the Alaska Railroad "so as best to aid in the development of the agricultural and mineral and other resources of Alaska." It was a laudable project, and if the railroad had not been built, the United States Smelting Refining and Mining operations would not be at Fairbanks today. However, to look at the present rates, you would never know that the road had been planned to "aid development." They date back to the depression when Congress, annoyed by the railroad's six years of million-dollar deficits, ordered that freight charges be upped 50 per cent and passenger fare raised to ten cents a mile. It was later lowered to six cents where it stands today, almost three times the average in the States. Many of the freight rates have been increased even further since then, including those on agricultural and mining machinery so vital to a frontier. (Unlike the railroads in the States, the Alaska Railroad can raise and lower its rates without giving prior notice to the Interstate Commerce Commission.) The machinery rates, however, are still below the level of the others, and there is less complaint about them than about the rate on Diesel oil, of which the mining industry ships in a much greater annual volume. Standard Oil lands it at Seward for eight cents, but since the railroad charges eleven cents just to haul it up to Fairbanks, the mines of the Interior cannot get it for less than twenty.

The Alaska Railroad's through rates are some 79 per cent higher than the local distance class rates of railroads in the northwest States, and comparing them with the through rates of a transcontinental, you find that the Alaska Railroad charges five times as much per mile to haul canned vegetables and clothing, seven times as much to haul fresh meat, and ten times as much to haul salt. Its local point-to-point rates are, of course, even more.

The people of Fairbanks dislike the railroad not only for its high rates but also for its slow service, and because its station agents can seldom tell them when the next train is going to run. (This is because the trains run to connect with the overcrowded boats whose schedules are constantly subject to change.) Cap Lathrop once got aboard with his baggage only to be told that he would have to get off, as the train was not leaving that day after all. For such episodes, as well as for the rates, the railroad's manager, Colonel Otto Ohlson, is indignantly attacked as a dictator, an imperious "Czar of the North."

Actually, the Colonel is an honest hard-working, hard-

swearing Swede who began as a Pennsylvania Railroad telegraph boy in 1893 and was a Northern Pacific division manager at the time that President Coolidge sent him to Alaska
fourteen years ago. He seems more annoyed than distressed
by all the resentment over his rates. The merchants, he says,
would never dream of passing on any reductions to the consumers. "Why does it cost a dollar to get a haircut in Fairbanks?" he asks. "Is that the freight, too? Who the devil are
the robbers?"

The truth is that ever since Colonel Ohlson went to
Alaska his whole attention has been directed toward one
thing—which does not happen to be the needs of the Territory. He is not personally responsible for this limited perspective; it is rather the fault of Congress itself which became
so impatient over the road's steady losses that there was some
talk of tearing up the track. Colonel Ohlson got instructions
to cut down the railroad's deficits, and when he left Washington in 1928 he told them it would take him ten years. It did—
almost to a day. He cut the operating ratio from 165 to 97,
and in 1938, for the first time, the railroad operated $76,703
in the black. He did an excellent job—the only trouble is that
it was an unsound project in the first place, since the frontier
region does not afford enough traffic to support a profitable
railroad. The normal inbound traffic is less than 150,000 tons
a year, of which two-thirds is local coal, and the outbound
traffic is almost nil.

Either the government had to subsidize the railroad, or it
had to take it out on the Alaskans. The Colonel's success was
bound to be at the expense of the Territory, and the government had only itself to blame when the Sourdough Express
("In Business Since '98") and other small truckers began
bringing produce up from the port of Valdez in summer over

the Richardson Highway. First, the railroad cut its competitive rates, raising them again as soon as the highway was blocked by the first winter snow. It also began operation of a special Brill car, speeding up its service on perishables from two days to eighteen hours. When the trucks continued to run, the Interior Department imposed a steep toll amounting to $9.27 a ton on all through freight, to be collected at a ferry-crossing on the highway. To this flagrant tactic the truckers responded in like vein, locking up the collector in the tollhouse and running boats across themselves, and the grand jury at Fairbanks refused to indict them. "If Mr. Ickes wants to be a dictator," one youthful truck-driver declared, "why doesn't he go over to Germany?" When it was rumored that the Interior Department had ordered an iron gate put across the road, more violence threatened; and the controversy was taken to court.

Much the same kind of Wild West battle took place when the *Discoverer,* the *Western Trader,* and other small boats began bringing cargo direct from Seattle to Anchorage, thus cutting the railroad out of a 114-mile haul from Seward. On one occasion the railroad ran a string of cars across the track so the boat-owner couldn't move his cargo off the dock. "Kids' play," says Colonel Ohlson who was "Outside" at the time; but he was so enraged at the merchants for ordering groceries on the boats that he opened a commissary for his employees in retaliation—no slight blow, for, next to the Army, his payroll is the biggest in Anchorage. Certain merchants are so fearful of his wrath that they place their orders under fictitious names. The Colonel estimates that the highway and boat competition has lost the railroad some $95,000; but this is trifling compared with what the controversy has lost the government in good will, to say nothing of the crimp which the high rates have put in local economic development.

Fortunately the War Department's new harbor project will lower operating costs and the Colonel plans to cut fares accordingly. "Tell the good people of the Interior to keep their shirts on," he booms. However, although the reduction as announced will be 30 per cent to Anchorage, to Fairbanks (where the freight cost grievance is worst) it will be only eight.

The Alaskan resentment against Mr. Ickes, however, is not entirely explained by the high-handed operation of the railroad. According to one leading Territorial official, "It springs from little things as well as big ones." Interior Alaskans complain most frequently about the high rates and the toll; but they also have a lot to say about Secretary Ickes himself, and his personal snubs to the people of the Territory when he visited it on his honeymoon trip in 1938. The stories have become legends, repeated over and over, and although they have doubtless been exaggerated in the telling, they represent a very real factor in political sentiment. Secretary Ickes, the Alaskans will tell you, "treated like school children" a group of Fairbanks citizens delegated to extend him the town's official welcome. Later, standing before a public gathering in Fairbanks, he told them what he would do if he were dictator of Alaska. When the assembled farmers of Matanuska asked him how he had enjoyed a dinner of home-grown vegetables, he replied, "When a woman shows you her baby, you don't like to tell her it's cross-eyed." In the course of a speech he made on his return to the States, he tried to refer to the capital of Alaska but was unable to remember its name. "What's the name of that place up there?" he asked.

The Alaskan frontier, like every other, is peopled by rugged individualists. The Alaskans resent federal interference, much as it is still resented by the backwoods mountaineers of Kentucky and Tennessee. They resent it as much—and more; for the Alaskan frontier has a special problem not found in the case of the others. After seventy-five long years it still lacks the status of a State, and the Alaskans still have no right to vote in Presidential elections. Lacking many of the political prerogatives of Americans Outside, they have developed a peculiar sensitivity to anything that smacks of condescension, as well as anything that smacks of authority. They are so sensitive in this respect that some of the federal officials in the Territory refer to their attitude as a "persecution complex." It is not difficult to imagine the impact of Secretary Ickes' positive statements and rough gibes on such a psychology. It is not difficult to imagine their reaction to his use, even in jest, of the word "dictator," and to his imposition of the steep highway toll in an effort to stop the operation of Alaskan trucks.

But when you have heard the story of the railroad and highway toll, you have heard the most important specific damage which the Alaskans claim to have suffered at the hands of the "bureaucrats." They have few others to name. While they are scornful of the confusion and overlapping of federal functions, and complain that decisions are too often made in Washington instead of on the ground, this in itself is hardly the stuff of which real bitterness is made.

The Alaskans certainly have no objection to the work of the post office, the coast guard, and all the other agencies which operate in the Territory as well as in the States; or, if they have one, it is only that they do not have enough funds for their northern work. For example, they have high praise for the work of Dr. Philip Smith of the Geological Survey. Since 1906 this distinguished geologist, wandering in high boots along the region's remote creeks and mountainsides, has made many friends among the Alaskans. He probably knows the region as well as any other living man, and few, if any, have met more of its lonely prospecting and trapping frontiersmen.

Alaskans along the coast likewise have praise for Regional Forester B. Frank Heintzleman. No sourdough has worried more about developing the region's resources than has Frank Heintzleman in his long years of effort to interest American paper interests in the southeastern forests. He is especially well liked, because the Forest Service allows its representatives a generous amount of local discretion, and he has an unusual amount of power to find out Alaskan problems and make decisions on the spot. Since the forests still remain virgin, the Service has little to do with trees; but the Alaskans enjoy the ski-jumps and shelters which the CCC, under Forest Service supervision, has built along the coastal mountains, the attractive docks and picnic grounds that have been put along the lakes, and the miles of prospectors' trails that have been built in mineralized regions of the forest domain.

One of the few important prohibitions placed on the legislature by the Organic Act of 1912 forbids it to pass any law affecting fish or game. All control is vested in the federal government. In the past, charges of corruption were made against the Bureau of Fisheries, especially during its operation under a political appointee named Frank T. Bell. Today, the Bureau has been merged into the Fish and Wildlife Service, and the National Director, huge, jovial Dr. Ira N. Gabrielson, is recognized as thoroughly honest and capable. There is still dissatisfaction about the control of trap-sites.

There is also an annual epidemic of complaints concerning the Service's strict regulations, yet it is conceded by salmon industry spokesmen as well as by Alaskans that the government brought back the salmon run when it was threatened with depletion.

Some Alaskans urge that the legislature be given control over the fish and game. When I asked an outstanding Alaskan whether he thought they should take over the salmon fisheries, he said, at first: "Certainly. War is being waged throughout the world for the extension of democratic self-government. Why shouldn't the Alaskans be given more of it?"

But then, frowning, and scratching his head, he looked out of his office window. Finally, he turned to me again with a candid half-smile and gave a different answer.

"Well," he said, "I mean in theory. But when you come right down to it, I'm afraid the legislature might not continue the enlightened conservation policy. I'm afraid we wouldn't have any fish left after a few years."

This appears to be the point of view of thoughtful Alaskans.

A unique and little-known Alaskan resource that was also saved by federal conservation is the fur-seal herd on the Pribilof Islands, two hundred and fifty miles north of Dutch Harbor in the middle of the Bering Sea. These islands are the summer breeding-grounds of more than 80 per cent of all the fur seals in the world, and people on boats approaching the fog-bound Pribilofs can usually hear the roar of animal noise "like the thunder of a city" for some time before they see the mist-shrouded shores.

When the federal government took over the management of the seal herd in 1910, it had been nearly depleted by pelagic killing and uncontrolled slaughter at the hands of the Russian and American monopolies. There were only some 132,000 animals left out of millions. But in thirty-two years of careful conservation management, the herd on the Pribilofs has increased again to over 2,338,000. Killings are confined exclusively to males. With Fish and Wildlife Service officials supervising, the taking of the skins is accomplished in expert production-line fashion by skillful resident Aleuts— descendants of the people moved to the islands by the Russians in the early days. Later, when the animals swim south on their annual migration, Coast Guard cutters solicitously patrol the movement, following the millions of bobbing heads through the ocean as far down as California. The skins are sent for dressing and dyeing to the Fouke Fur Company in St. Louis, one of the only two companies in the world that have mastered the secret process involved. They are then sold at auction, and the proceeds are turned over to the United States Treasury. Since the government took over management of the Pribilof herd, the gross sales have totaled nearly $25,000,000.

The regulation of Alaska game, although it remains technically a legal function of the federal government, is carried out with the active participation of leading Alaskans, and since the inauguration of this set-up in 1925, the Alaska Game Commission (a Division of the Fish and Wildlife Service) has become the outstanding example of successful cooperation between the federal government and the Territory. While the executive officer, popular young Frank Dufresne, is technically a federal official he has lived in Alaska for twenty-one years. He knows it well, having covered much of the Territory by dog team, on foot, and on slow boat, working on reindeer grazing investigations and bear and moose census surveys, and other such assignments. The other four members of the commission are oldtime Alaskans: Earl Ohmer, the Petersburg "shrimp king" and fur farmer; Frank Williams, who runs a trading post at St. Michael and has lived in Alaska since 1896; "Andy" Simons of the Kenai peninsula, famous big-game guide, who has lived there since 1905; and John Hajdukovich, guide, trapper, and prospector of the upper Tanana region, who has been in Alaska since 1903. Not once since its organization in 1925 has any federal official vetoed a regulation proposed by this sourdough Commission.

There is probably no federal agency that is more essential to Alaska than the Office of Indian Affairs. Without its educational and medical work the condition of its native Alaskans would be even worse than it is today. While the white Alaskans are unusually democratic among themselves, their attitude toward the Indians is deplorable—almost reminiscent of the Southerners' attitude toward the Negro—and they are only too glad to have the federal government assume the burden of the natives' needs.

In this case, it must be noted, Secretary Ickes is far more concerned with Alaskan well-being than are most of the white Alaskans themselves. The Secretary has called the Eskimos and Indians "Alaska's greatest resource," and he recognizes the fact that here is a resource in large degree unknown and undeveloped. There are many stories current in the Territory about the extraordinary mechanical skill of the Eskimos; about the almost uncanny facility with which they can take a watch or an engine apart and put it back together again. They should make excellent aviation mechanics. There is one native out on the Aleutian Islands who can repair an engine when it stumps the best white mechanic. Native skill of this kind is much discussed among the white population of Alaska—but always as if it were an interesting and rather remote curiosity, never as if it were a real asset to the Territory itself. Secretary Ickes has taken an active interest in educational and economic opportunity for the Indians and Eskimos and however much his other administration of Alaska may be criticized, in this case he is attempting to meet one of the region's gravest problems. The Indian Affairs office operates 122 day schools and three boarding schools (the most widely scattered system in the world, excepting Russia). Over 6,500 children attend these schools (compared to four thousand attending school before the New Deal Administration); and while illiteracy is still high in some of the more remote regions of Alaska, most of the younger generation along the coasts can read and write.

The office also operates seven hospitals at remote points, like Barrow and Kanakanak and Unalaska; and maintains a number of itinerant doctors and nurses who travel long distances by dogsled or in native ski boats to give assistance to isolated settlements. Some forty-five villages have been organized and have received loans under the Indian Reorganization Act, and the government has instituted an arts and crafts program, helping the Indians with the marketing of their parkas, mukluks and ivory work.

Symbolically, it was the federal government, not the Alaskans, that saved the Indian totem poles when they were falling into disrepair. The Indians were provided federal funds for the work. A year was spent studying paint colors, and the job was painstakingly accomplished down to the last bright raven beak. As a result, one of Alaska's unique cultural contributions has been saved and interest in totem carving has been revived among the younger Indians.

Most of the federal activity in Alaska has been of great

benefit to the Alaskans and the home rule issue is not the basic one; but that issue is nevertheless a real one to some extent. An outstanding complaint is the fact that they do not have the right to choose their own Governor. Back in 1928 they went so far as to conduct an election, choosing a Juneau businessman, Cash Cole; but this was silently ignored by Calvin Coolidge, and they have not tried it since.

The Governor of Alaska lives in a white-pillared colonial mansion in the capital town of Juneau. His legal position has long been an unhappy one. While he is the nearest thing to an administrative head that the Territory has, the legal set-up in peacetime makes it difficult for him to function as such. It is his duty, on one hand, to see "that the laws enacted for said Territory are enforced"—a difficult assignment in view of the fact that he has little control of the U.S. Marshals and Deputy Marshals who are authorized to enforce justice. He is also ordered to see that the Territorial officers "faithfully discharge their duties"—yet he has little control over these officers, who can outvote him on many of the local administrative boards. On the other hand, it is his duty to represent "the interests of the United States within the Territory"—yet he has little control over the large collection of federal officials operating in Alaska. Although they cooperate with the Governor in an informal fashion, most of them report back to Washington rather than to him. The Governor's position is rendered unhappier still because the Alaskans resent the appointment of an Outsider from Washington.

On his way up to take charge of Alaska in December, 1939, Governor Ernest Gruening met the late Frank Cotter, beloved sourdough journalist, in Seattle.

"How do you think I will get along with the Alaskans?" the new Governor asked.

"You won't," said Cotter, "especially if you tell them how

to run things. They don't want to be bossed by anybody from Outside."

In one sense Frank Cotter's words were prophetic. The modern tax program that the Governor proposed to the 1941 Territorial legislature was defeated in its entirety. Almost from the start Gruening's relations with the Alaskans were difficult. At times they were stormy. Although Alaska had had twelve governors before him, although it had seen plenty of turbulent politics, it is safe to say that it had never experienced the kind of conflict that has occurred under the administration of Ernest Gruening.

Some of this, however, is to the Governor's credit. A great many more factors were involved than the one mentioned by Frank Cotter. The historic legislative battle of 1941 is worth analysis, for the issues, and the outcome, tell much about the Alaskans and about the complex relationship of political and economic forces in the Territory.

Ernest Gruening is the first governor to try to put through a tax program to meet Alaska's needs, and even many of his enemies will admit in private that he is the most intelligent executive Alaska has ever had.

Gruening is well known as a journalist and a scholar. The son of a New York doctor, he went to Harvard, graduated from Harvard Medical School with honors in 1912, and was assigned to the surgical staff of the Boston City Hospital. However, he soon decided that he was more interested in newspaper work, and during the next ten years he edited numerous papers and magazines, including the Boston *Traveler* and *Journal*, the New York *Tribune* and *Nation*. In 1924 he was national director of publicity for the La Follette Progressive campaign. Interested in inter-American relations, he conducted campaigns in the columns of his papers against the military occupation of Haiti and the intervention of the marines in Nicaragua. He spent two years in Mexico and wrote an outstanding book about it. In 1933 President Roosevelt sent him to South America as adviser to the American delegation to the Pan American Conference, and two years later the President appointed him Director of the Interior Department's new Division of Territories and Island Possessions. His record, in general, has been that of a liberal—although he has been criticized by progressives in Puerto Rico and in the States for the way in which he dealt with the affairs of that Island.

Since Governor Gruening took office in Juneau's massive Federal Building, he has worked hard for Alaska. When the Alaskans failed to get their fair share of the construction jobs at the bases, he went to bat for them with the Navy and got results. When the steamship companies raised their rates steeply to cover increased wartime costs he termed it an "outrage" and flew to Washington to testify that such an increase would work great hardship on the region. When the construction of a highway to Alaska was delayed even after war began, he argued doggedly and vehemently with Washington generals and officials. Gruening's close acquaintance with Washington has helped him to get increased federal funds to meet Alaska's needs; and he is alert to a vast variety of the region's problems.

No sourdough appreciates Alaska's scenic country any more than its Governor. As he flies across the vast distances between towns, he never gets tired of looking down on the majestic Alaskan wilderness or taking color shots of mountain and sea and tundra. With Mrs. Gruening (a Vassar graduate—the former Dorothy Elizabeth Smith of Norwood, Massachusetts), he goes on long hikes in the wild country back of Juneau. Sometimes they take a boat and go salmon-fishing along the fjords of the Inside Passage, and go swim-

ming in its spruce-fringed waters; and they play tennis at
the town's Evergreen Bowl courts which lie at the foot
of towering, boulder-like mountains. Appreciating Alaska's
painted totem poles as a unique cultural contribution, he was
so shocked when he heard that some were rotting with age
that he made personal trips to remote Indian settlements to
take pictures proving that funds were needed for their repair.
One of the biggest and brightest totem poles in the Territory, built by natives on a WPA project, stands on the lawn
in front of his white colonial mansion.

The Governor and Mrs. Gruening entertain frequently.
Mrs. Gruening is a gracious hostess, and there is a combination of cool distinction and friendly informality about the
gatherings. Although the ladies come decked in evening
gowns, the men, who are allowed to wear what they please,
frequently appear in business suits. The crowd usually consists of government officials and their wives, with a scattering
of townspeople like Dr. and Mrs. Robert Simpson, owners of
the famous Nugget Shop, and Mr. and Mrs. Robert Schoet-
tler, managers of the Baranof Hotel. In winter and fall, and
even on cool summer evenings, bright fires are kept blazing in
the large fireplaces contrasting with the gloomy fog and rain
outside. As everywhere else in Alaska, there is a sense of
motion and suspense because of "the planes"; often enough
Mrs. Gruening must rearrange her guest list at the last minute because "that Unemployment Commission crowd is
grounded at Whitehorse" or "the girl from the Forest Service
decided to fly Out this afternoon."

If the gathering is a large one (and it frequently is), the
guests dine informally at card tables in the elegant white-
paneled ballroom, lined with bright water colors by federal
artists. While the American flag and the blue, star-spangled

Territorial banner stand in state beside the grand piano, the atmosphere is much like that in any other well-appointed large home back in the States. Talking and laughing across bouquets of perennials or roses from Mrs. Gruening's garden, the guests often begin their meal with an Alaskan fish course. The food is excellent and plentiful; and later, as the room is cleared and the radio turned on for dancing, a huge bowl of punch is served in the living room. However, even as the Governor passes out after-dinner cigars, there is a subtle uneasiness in the air; and when I was in Juneau shortly before war began, I found that the politics of the provincial town were full of bitterness.

As I danced with the Governor on one of those evening occasions shortly after my arrival in Alaska, I remember remarking that Alaska's political situation seemed very complex.

"There's nothing complex about it," he told me, "once you understand the reasons behind it."

More time than I had at my disposal would be necessary to pass judgment on the maze of detailed claims and counterclaims of the 1941 legislative battle. However, there are certain basic aspects of that fight that are very striking to the reporter learning about it for the first time. In view of the opportunity I had for intensive interviews with federal and Territorial officials and with a variety of people in Alaska's larger towns, my impressions may be worth recording.

When President Roosevelt appointed Ernest Gruening to Alaska, Gruening proposed to the Alaskan legislature that it enact a modern tax system to meet Territorial needs.

"Alaska," he told the legislators as they convened, "has enriched the nation; but it has done relatively little for itself. The time has come when an increasing proportion of that wealth should be kept in Alaska for the further development, progress and improvement of Alaska and the Alaskans . . . This is no narrowly exclusive policy. It is, however, an effort to realize for Alaska a new era in which Alaska shall be less and less a mining camp to which thousands come seasonally to extract what they can and take it all 'down below.' It is time for us to exhibit a greater and more enlightened self-interest in terms of the people of Alaska. And when I say the people of Alaska, I mean those who want to live here and stay here and create here and build here."

Alaska is the most lightly taxed entity under the American flag. Its taxes are less than half those of Nevada, which boasts of its low rate. Nevada, producing goods and services totaling some $75,000,000, raises roughly $7,000,000 in State and local taxes. Alaska, with an income of roughly $90,000,000, collects (including unemployment contributions) only $3,-000,000. If Alaska had a tax system equal in revenue-raising power to that prevailing in the States, the Territory and its incorporated cities would receive some $9,000,000—over three times present receipts.

Alaska has no net income tax worth mention, either personal or corporate. The salmon industry, which pays a gross tax on its pack, finds its burden far lighter than in Oregon or Washington. Libby, McNeill and Libby, in 1941, had gross sales of $7,804,600 but paid only $82,800.

The gold industry also pays taxes on its gross sales, figured at only 3 per cent with a $20,000 exemption. When gold was revalued in the early years of the Roosevelt administration, the mining companies got a 69 per cent price boost; and in view of this windfall their burden is especially slight. In 1941 United States Smelting Refining and Mining Company paid only $194,193 although its gross production was $6,585,000.

There is no tax on property—except for a small one within the limits of incorporated towns. Only part of the large Alaska Juneau property is taxed, and the extensive United States Smelting operations outside Fairbanks get off scot-free. So do the increasing number of Alaskans who have moved into houses beyond town limits, although they continue to benefit from the publicly maintained schools and roads.

Although there is a tax on liquor, the Territory has little else but an antiquated maze of small license levies and the $5 school tax paid by men between the ages of 21 and 50. While there is a tax on mercantile establishments, it is very slight. In 1941, Standard Oil of California paid only $6,600 on gross sales of $3,956,800; and the Northern Commercial Company only $6,350 on gross sales of $2,857,000.

"What of it?" some of the Governor's critics asked. "Why raise taxes when there is no need?" One of their hand-outs which purported to give a critical analysis of the Governor's proposals, contended: "It has never been considered sound public financial policy to raise large amounts of revenue merely as a moral exercise for the good of the taxpayer."

But as the 1941 legislature convened, the Territorial Budget Board informed them that they faced a deficit of $600,000 in the ordinary running expenses of their government. The University of Alaska at Fairbanks, crowded into a cluster of small structures, was turning away students for lack of funds. There was urgent need for a new building to house the federal and Territorial agencies operating in Juneau. The Pioneers' Home at Sitka had a constant waiting list of thirty or forty men in need of shelter and medical care. The Alaskans have always complained that they do not have enough roads. With the roaring defense program under way in the Territory, children of construction workers and of Army and Navy personnel were arriving in such numbers that the schools did not have enough desks to accommodate them. At the Navy base town of Sitka there were twice as many children crowded into the buildings as the school was built to hold. Some of the classes were held in the basement and pupils in the science laboratory could not write because they had to meet standing up. Schools in several other boom towns had similar conditions.

There was no hospital of any kind at Sitka, except for limited facilities at the Pioneers' Home. All children born in the town were delivered at private homes. There had never been enough hospitals in Alaska, and now, with the war program, these and a great many other community facilities were acutely needed. As Jack Conway, the Mayor of Sitka, remarked: "At least, we had a town here. That's more than they had in some places." Kodiak's population had quadrupled; most of its shacks were without electric lights, and there was no sewage system. While some federal funds had been appropriated for the defense communities in the Territory they did not begin to meet the needs. Gruening told the legislators:

"The growth of population has created new problems. Present facilities in school accommodations, in communications, in public utilities, in housing, in public health, in roads, in many other ways which possibly were adequate for a population of fifty-odd thousand are not adequate for a population of over 80,000. That is what our population will be before the end of this year, and from that point, it will move rapidly higher."

Finally, apart from the Territory's requirements, it faced the problem of building armories for the newly organized National Guard. Although the federal government was

financing the equipment and payroll, War Department officials took the position that Alaska, like the States and other
Territories and possessions, should pay for the armories. "It
would seem unthinkable," Gruening told the legislators at
their opening session, "that Alaska would not do at least a
part of what other Territories, Hawaii, and Puerto Rico, had
done much earlier and on a larger scale."

The defense construction program in Alaska had not only
brought additional needs; it had also brought additional revenue which could be tapped to meet them. As the legislature convened, contractors were working on $70,000,000
worth of Army and Navy construction; in the towns near the
bases the business of local merchants and bankers was boom-
ing in a "second Gold Rush." But none of this gold was going
into the Territorial Treasury to help supply Alaska's mounting needs.

"If we are wise," said the Governor, "we shall be able to
profit immensely by this bonanza which has come and is
continuing to come to us in the shape of more people and
more activities."

Governor Gruening proposed that a modern tax system be
substituted for the antiquated hodge-podge under which the
Territory was operating. The rates that he suggested were
moderate, and have seldom, if ever, been attacked by his
opponents. He proposed a 2 per cent net income tax on individuals (with a special exemption for residents); a 4 per cent
net income tax on corporations, and a property tax of ten mills.
This was the gist of his program. He also proposed that the
gold industry continue to pay its gross tax, to be considered
as a severance tax since it was depleting a national resource
that could never be restored.

The legislature, which had full power to enact such a

program or to revise it any way it might see fit, killed it in its
entirety. Yet appropriations came to at least $600,000 more
than the funds available for them. The legislators declined
to appropriate anything for armories, or for a new Territorial
building. They refused needed funds for the University.
Finally, they shirked the problem of mounting community
needs; and as work on the new bases is completed, hundreds
of thousands of dollars which might have been raised by
taxing the construction payroll are irrevocably lost to the
Territory.

Who were the men in the Alaska legislature? At least
half of them were small-town merchants—the proprietors
of small hotels and theaters and drugstores and pool halls and
drygoods shops. Many had a stake in the smaller placer mines
of the Interior region. Most of them were men of integrity,
with the welfare of the Territory at heart, and it is worthy of
note that the majority of the House, despite the high-running
prejudice of the 1941 legislature, voted in favor of the Governor's income tax bill which was later defeated in the Senate.
While some members of the House worked against it, it was a
small group of men in the Senate, headed by baldish, elderly
Senator O. D. Cochran of Nome, that defeated the Governor's program. Senator Cochran, the local attorney for the
United States Smelting Refining and Mining Company, frequently orated in old-school fashion against Gruening's proposal, and when the income tax bill was introduced into the
Senate, he voted to throw it out without benefit of a reading.

Another Senator who voted against the Governor was C. H.
LaBoyteaux, popularly known as "Alabam," an oldtimer from
the mining town of Livengood, who refused to wear a neck-
tie during the entire session. He also refused to read the tax

bill, which he criticized as "too long." When Alabam campaigned for office, he distributed posters of himself wearing a striped criminal's shirt. "WANTED," the caption announced in large black letters. When elected, he sent out a new set entitled, "CAPTURED." Alabam set such a high record for rugged individualism in politics that some of his constituents wired him complaining that he had neglected their interests. "You mind your own business back there," he is reported to have replied, "and I'll mind my business here in Juneau." Most of the legislators did not carry individualism to the same degree as Alabam. Like Senator Cochran, he represents an extreme rather than a type. Yet it may safely be said that the frontiersman's dislike for interference ran strong among the members of the Alaska legislature, as did the peculiar blend of sensitivity and resentment toward federal dictation that is characteristic of Alaskan political psychology.

The fact that Gruening was an Outsider was indisputably a factor operating against his program. Even before he arrived in Juneau, objections were raised against him. The fact that he hailed from the much-disliked Interior Department made it that much worse. The Alaskans took to calling him an "Ickes-ite"—which is amusing, to say the least, since it is well known in Washington that there has been no love lost between the two men. Had the federal government appointed an Alaskan to the Governor's office, a large part of the difficulty might have disappeared. It is notable, in this connection, that no antagonism exists toward "Bob" Bartlett, Secretary of Alaska, although he is, like the Governor, a federal appointee. Bartlett, who grew up in Alaska, attending its University, working as a reporter in Fairbanks and gold-mining in the Interior, has not only the respect but the warm regard of Alaskans.

The Governor's own blunt personality was another factor contributing to the controversy. Many Alaskans felt that he condescended to them and attempted to give them orders. Some of them complained that he brought in an "Outside expert" to cram the tax program down their throats ready-made. The Governor replies that the legislature had full power to make any revision in the program; he had secured one of the outstanding tax experts in the country, free of charge to the Territory, to assist them in framing any laws they might desire. But critics felt that he should have consulted Territorial officials before drawing up the program, and that he was completely uncompromising in his position on the armories, insisting on a cost far higher than the region could reasonably pay.

Governor Gruening, by most accounts, is no diplomat; and in dealing with Territorial officials and legislators he made known his wishes (and his criticisms) in no uncertain terms. This is, of course, the prerogative of the executive arm of the government. But in view of the Alaskan allergy to anything resembling dictation, it is not surprising that his manner should have contributed to ill-feeling and misunderstanding.

"Misunderstanding" seems the best word to describe the situation that existed between the Governor and the Alaskans.

"It's too bad," one of the Alaskan Senators told me, as he sorted merchandise behind the counter of his small store; "the Governor is on the side of the people, and a lot of them don't even know it."

This misunderstanding played directly into the hands of absentee business interests, who were well-represented in Juneau on the occasion of the 1941 legislative session. The tax battle was not a simple clash between the Governor and the Alaskans. It was a three-cornered affair; and in his efforts to install a modern tax program in Alaska, the Governor had to take on a second and very potent adversary—namely, the Lobby of the gold and salmon industries. In this situation, ironically, home-rule sentiment played into the hands of absentee business interests, and the Alaskans themselves were the losers.

The situation was well summarized at the session's close in the Juneau Women's Club edition of the *Alaska Daily Press,* a thoroughly respectable paper carrying advertisements from the town's leading banks and merchants. As the Senators and Representatives boarded their boats and planes for remote towns scattered through the region, Mildred Hermann, competent bustling lawyer who edits an occasional women's club edition of the *Press,* declared editorially:

> The Lobby has triumphed again . . . One by one, revenue measures were sent to the limbo, under the expert manipulation of the most efficient and most extensive lobby ever assembled in Juneau.

These are strong words, but no stronger than the Governor's as he issued a special message to the Alaskan people. Assailing the gold and cannery interests, he remarked that Adolf Hitler "could have found here in Alaska recently a confirmation of [his] caustic condemnation of democracies." He continued:

> Time will prove him wrong. Neither Alaska nor any part of our beloved United States will be controlled by the penny-pinching pretended patriots, by the lobbyists whose flag is the dollar-sign and who at all times in their methods and morals are the enemies of the democratic process.

There was only one registered business lobbyist at the legislature—"Judge" W. C. Arnold of Ketchikan, able counsel to

the canned salmon industry. But that others were busy in
the galleries and hotel rooms is a fact that no one in Juneau
would attempt to deny. In talking politics with numerous
people in the other towns as well, I found few who did not
believe that the gold and salmon lobby, working along with
a few small entrepreneurs, had been a major factor in defeat-
ing the Governor's program. Not the only factor, to be sure;
but a major one. If you ask Governor Gruening whether he
does not think Alaskans should have more say in their own
affairs, he replies sharply, "Why *don't* they?"

While some of the Alaskan legislators who opposed the
Governor's program may have sincerely felt that they were
being "dominated" by the federal government, the real
domination seems to have been of quite another kind. Freedom from bureaucratic control became a catchword in a kind
of sham battle, obscuring the basic issues much as States'
rights appeals have served, on occasion, to obscure them here.
It was, fundamentally, a repetition of the familiar struggle
between business and government, and perhaps no speech of
the session was more symbolic than the one made by Edward
F. Medley, Seattle attorney for Alaska's own Cap Lathrop,
when he told the discomfited legislators: "The Territory is
not ready for this bill. It is like putting a Tuxedo on an infant."

It is a significant fact that the Alaskan legislature, although
most of its members were Democrats, passed almost no laws
stemming from the New Deal administration. This was true
not only in the 1941 session under Gruening but in all the
previous sessions since Roosevelt took office. In some cases
it lost federal grants because it refused to appropriate the
necessary matching funds.

Although Alaska is a "workingman's country," since few

of the owners of its major industries choose to reside there, the Alaska legislature has failed to enact such progressive labor legislation for the protection of labor as has been passed by many states: it has passed no general eight-hour-day law, no wage-and-hour law, no Labor Relations Act. The 1941 session killed a bill to extend the benefits of the workmen's compensation act; and although it did pass a bill setting up a Territorial Department of Labor, its enforcement provisions were so weak that its effectiveness was slight.

Considering the unstable pattern of the Alaskan economic scene, it is hardly surprising that political maturity has not been achieved. The pattern is much the same as that of the copper-dominated legislatures of the sparsely populated western States, with the added factor that functioning business, as well as government, controls have operated from far distant points and Gold Rush transient attitudes have continued strong. Only recently have the Alaskans begun to realize their power to improve conditions in the Territory by a greater measure of self-government. One of the most promising developments is the increased political activity of the Alaskan labor movement; and as the legislature becomes more representative of the ordinary working people of Alaska, concerned with their needs and wishes, many of the problems of the Territory's pride and politics will automatically be resolved.

XI

YESTERDAY AND TOMORROW

ONLY IN THE months since the Pearl Harbor attack have most Americans been more than dimly conscious of this country's outlying Territories and Possessions, and then chiefly in terms of beach-heads and fox-holes. Yet the present conflict has deeper implications. As war progresses, social changes are occurring under its impact. Democracy is changing as it fights. As the people of our exposed and outlying possessions face bombs and gunfire on our account, our record and our responsibilities need reappraising, and it is only fitting that the problems of these lands are gaining fuller recognition from the man on the street and from the government itself.

The United States has never had a thoroughgoing policy for Alaska. Its problems have not been considered or handled as a whole by authorities in Washington. Instead, the Territory's management has been left in the hands of a variety of agencies, each of which administers its Alaskan office as an incidental part of its nationwide operation. There have been several attempts at coordination, including an inter-departmental Alaska Committee in Washington which is headed by the Interior Department's Director of Territories and Island Possessions, but none, to date, has been adequate. Appropriations for Alaska are passed in a hit-or-miss fashion, usually as minor items in general bills. Some federal laws have been extended to Alaska, but others have not. As a result, although many of the agencies do excellent work in

178

Alaska, the pattern of government activity as a whole has long been planless and confused.

Red tape and inter-departmental friction are, of course, time-worn American customs and hardly confined to Alaska. But they are more harmful there. Alaska is remote, and it is faced with many unique problems, and the solution of these problems is hardly simplified when it is administered by a large number of agencies each of which must refer its decisions back to Washington thousands of miles away. Although over 98 per cent of all the resources are under federal ownership, and the sparsely populated region must rely on the federal government for most of its needs, the Territory has no vote in Congress and, being "nobody's constituency," it has frequently been pushed aside in the turmoil of the Washington free-for-all.

From the very start the Americans in Alaska have been pushed around by a multiplicity of government departments. As described by the outstanding history of our early rule of the Territory,* back in 1868 (the year after the region passed into our hands) the new citizens at Sitka received a series of prompt discouragements from Washington:

The Department of Interior informed them that their claims to the townsite were illegal; and the Department of War ordered the discharge of all civilians in military pay. The Treasury Department sent up a representative in the person of a collector of customs who had the unfortunate distinction of being Alaska's sole civil officer and of bearing a commission to treat Alaska as an Indian country.

------

* *Alaska: A History of Its Administration, Exploitation and Industrial Development During Its First Half-Century Under the Rule of the United States,* by Jeannette Paddock Nichols, Ph. D. Cleveland: The Arthur H. Clark Co., 1924. Reprinted by permission of the publisher.

Despite the frequent appeals of the Alaskans, no move was made in Washington to set up a civil government for the region either that year or for sixteen years thereafter. For part of that time it came under the jurisdiction of the War Department; later it was taken over by the Navy which was followed in turn by the Treasury. None of them gave it much attention. When a civil administration was finally established,

the incoming government, as personified in the servants of the Departments of Justice and Interior, found its relations with the former de facto government of the Treasury and Navy decidedly strained, because the Organic Act gave the former all the responsibility for good order and left in possession of the latter the instruments existing for maintaining it. The Governor, the judge, and several others were shortly found taking refuge in Washington, leaving the territory to its former device of running itself.

Not until the turn of the century, when Congress was reminded of the Territory's existence by the hectic excitement of the Gold Rush, was Alaska given a code of civil and criminal law. Not until 1912 was it given the right to elect a local legislature. All through these decades the Alaskans were gathering in town-meeting fashion and sending appeals to Washington for some kind of recognition. Back in 1868 the citizens of Sitka, fearing an uprising of the natives, went so far as to appeal to Canada for protection, complaining:

We have made application to our government for protection and aid, and thus far it has taken no notice of our application.

The Canadian government responded by sending a man-of-war to Sitka, which was followed at a later date by the U.S.S. *Jamestown.* On another occasion a mass meeting at Valdez sent a resolution to Washington declaring "on behalf of 60,000 American citizens of Alaska, who are denied the right of representation in any form, we demand, in mass meeting assembled, that Alaska be annexed to Canada."

In the days of Russian rule the native Aleuts had a saying: "God is high and the Czar far away"; years later the Nome *Nugget* echoed the cry, declaring: "God is afar off, and it's a long way to Washington." Beginning in 1890, the Alaskans held a series of "Non-Partisan" conventions for the purpose of passing memorials and electing delegates to be sent to Washington. The first one grew out of a Fourth of July miners' mass meeting, and was called "for the purpose of taking some action toward the procurement of the recognition and representation of this Territory by the United States Government." The convention, held in Juneau, complained:

We are denied representation in Congress. Our jurisprudence is distortion. Our judicial system is faulty. We have no title to land. We have no voice or control of public schools. Our liquor law is obnoxious. Our postal system is inefficient. Our government buildings are in decay or altogether lacking.

This gathering sent a delegate to Washington, but he was not seated. Several Territorial Clubs were organized and two additional Non-Partisan Conventions were held, passing memorials and collecting funds to send representatives to Congress. Not until 1906, thirty-nine years after the region passed into American hands, was the Alaskan delegate awarded formal recognition in Washington.

Such a degree of indifference no longer exists and, as the previous chapter describes, Alaska has received an increased measure of recognition and constructive help from the federal government, particularly under the Roosevelt administration. However, decisions vital to its economic structure and to its civilian morale are still rendered by a variety of bureaus and departments without over-all plan or coordination.

A few recent events illustrate the haphazard nature of our territorial management.

When Jesse Jones announced the availability of war damage compensation in a press release, which he later said could be considered the equivalent of an insurance policy, it covered only property damage within the borders of the continental United States. It was not until protests had been made by Delegate Dimond, Delegate Samuel King of Hawaii, and Secretary Ickes that the benefits were extended to cover property in the Territories and Possessions. As first proclaimed, the insurance left unprotected that American property which is most exposed to destruction; it left financially insecure those citizens who are already facing the greatest personal danger. The wrong, in this case, was quickly righted; but, generally speaking, Alaska has often suffered because important matters affecting its economic and social life have been forgotten or handled in an offhand fashion by Washington officials, busy with their general work.

The second action, while less shocking than the first, caused considerable damage in Alaska before it was corrected. A few weeks after the Pearl Harbor attack the Maritime Commission's Division of Rates and Regulations, without notice, and without holding any hearings, announced that rates on the steamship lines serving Alaska would be subject to an immediate increase of 45 per cent. Delegate Dimond knew nothing about the increase until it was granted. His first news of the action came in the form of a telegram from Alaska. The increase, he learned, had been allowed the steamship lines principally to cover the costs of war-risk insurance. At that time no government agency was authorized to write this insurance, and thus the burden was to be thrown entirely on the steamship lines, which had been given permission to pass it on to their shippers and passengers. This meant, of course, that much of it would be borne ultimately by the people living in Alaska.

Owing to the Territory's almost complete dependence on the water route, such a drastic increase was bound to have far-reaching effects on the economy. Alaska's high living costs had mounted sharply since the defense program had started there. Delegate Dimond estimated that the increase would in one year take more money out of the pockets of the people of Alaska than the whole revenues of the Territorial government for the same period. Numerous complaints arrived by wire and letter from Alaska, the Office of Price Administration petitioned for reopening the case, and the Maritime Commission called hearings to reconsider its action.

Governor Gruening pointed out that the increase ran directly contrary to the government's price stabilization policy. Mr. J. C. Rettie, Alaska Counselor to the National Resources Planning Board, testified that the average Juneau family of four was currently paying some $42 a year in ocean freight costs on its food alone, and that it would be forced under the new rates to pay $60; that for families living in cities farther north the load would rise from $65 to $95. Mr. Rettie also noted that one-half the population of Alaska consists of Eskimos, Indians, and Aleuts, and that a large proportion of these natives, who already have one of the lowest standards of living under the American flag, were faced with a serious situation because of the wartime curtailment of the salmon industry on which many of them made their living. Calling this policy of shifting war costs to Alaska "dreary imperialism," he dramatized the appeal that could readily be made to these Alaskans by fifth columnists:

Look what white man do. War come. Big war risk insurance. Big bonus for crew of steamships. Steamship companies making big money. Pay big excess profit tax. White man's government pay these war costs? No. Merchants and white traders pay these? No. You pay these? Yes. Your families go to States when bombs fall in Alaska? No! No, you stay right here. Take all this and die.

The rate dispute, Mr. Rettie told the Examiner, was

not a simple clash of economic interests which must be adjusted. . . . You have before you a case that involves the economy and civilian morale of the Territory of Alaska—undoubtedly one of the most vital and critical of the remaining outposts which we possess.

The Commission, examining Alaska Steam's books, found that the 1941 earnings exceeded 11 per cent of fair value of its property. The Commission ordered the company to submit a new tariff which would lower earnings to 6 per cent, also requiring that the surcharge be reduced to 25 and 20 per cent, and that special low rates granted to a Navy contractor be discontinued.

Another recent disheartening instance of lack of federal coordination was the delay in providing recreational centers for service men in several of the towns. Despite the unusually serious problem of troop morale in Alaska before the war, caused by the lonely isolation of the region and the almost complete lack of recreational facilities of any kind, progress on the centers was slow; and a large factor in this delay was red tape and ritual involved between the Federal Works Agency, the Federal Security Agency, the United Service Organizations and the Army—with final authority for many decisions resting far away in Washington. A legal tangle kept the new center at Ketchikan closed even after its completion.

Perhaps the most important failure in recent years was the

slowness in increasing the small output of the Matanuska colony to meet the Army's food requirements. Although the Matanuska Coop's sales of fresh milk and dairy products quadrupled during 1941, production of other foods increased only slightly in spite of the arrival of thousands of potential new consumers at nearby Fort Richardson. Five thousand cleared acres were out of use in 1941, many farmers were off working at the Fort, and not until war began did the colony formulate a plan for substantial production increase.

Although the government deserves full credit for establishing an agricultural colony in Alaska, management of the project has been spasmodic, lacking a long-range plan. "You can't set up a thing like that and expect it to grow like a mushroom," one leading Alaskan told me. The government has been criticized for many things: for bringing up reliefers not qualified to farm; for extending them over-generous credit at the outset, and clamping down too stiffly later on; for allowing them only forty acres apiece, too little for crop rotation; finally for a ruling passed in 1939 which required the farmers to sign contracts forgoing the right to ownership of their farms even after their debts should be paid in full. (Average indebtedness: $5,000 to $7,000.) This last policy caused a furore among the colonists, and a secret organization called "The Order of Iceworms" began to issue a series of mimeographed bulletins attacking the government's policies. The fight became even more bitter when the government instituted eviction suits against some of the colonists who, in a gesture of defiance, refused to make payments on their debts.

Despite all the money that has been spent at Matanuska, no effort has been made to help the farmers with a long-range marketing program. According to the manager of the

Matanuska Valley Cooperating Association, "Uncertainty has been the big problem, not soil or climate." One of the most highly respected farmers in the valley stated: "The colonists feel insecure. They would be pleased if they could sign definite contracts with the government."

In contrast to the generous loans advanced to the original settlers, credit was not available at less than 8 per cent at the time of war's outbreak. Not until after war started were Farm Security Administration loans extended to Alaska. The colonists also complained that the Army was shipping in its food from the States at low rates with which they could not compete. Since Matanuska is a federal project, it was to be expected that early action would be taken in Washington to develop it to its utmost as a source of military supply. But in this case, as in many others, there was no coordinated plan.

In the opinion of some outstanding officials concerned with Alaska, an efficient government structure is only part of what has been lacking in our management of the Territory. Their criticism goes further. While the work of many of the federal agencies has been excellent, they feel that it has been severely limited by the inadequacy of Congressional appropriations. The past record, they feel, has been not only one of confusion, but also one of neglect.

A dramatic example of federal indifference toward Alaska was the failure to provide effective fire control in the Interior region. Pilots flying the inland routes in summertime were frequently forced off their routes by clouds of heavy smoke. Looking down, they saw flames sweeping across vast areas, with no effort made to put them out. As described in a 1936 article by Regional Forester B. Frank Heintzleman:

The effects of fire far transcend in importance the combined results of all other agencies which work toward the depletion of the valuable land resources of the Territory . . . Not uncommonly a fire will rage for many weeks and extend over hundreds of square miles before being checked by natural barriers such as rivers or by the coming of the fall rains.

In 1935 a fire in the Kvichavak River section, burning for more than two months in brush, grass, tundra, and scrub timber, covered an area estimated at 1,000 square miles in a region formerly teeming with wild life of every sort.

He estimated that tens of millions of acres have been fire-swept at least once, and much of this area two or three times, since the turn of the century. These blazes have occurred in areas adjacent to towns, as well as in the more remote regions. In 1938 a committee of local citizens complained that "fires have run rampant from time to time in and through the timber adjacent to and in the vicinity of Anchorage." The following year, the Interior Department instituted an Alaskan Fire Control Service.

The federal government, in recent years, has spent an annual sum ranging from $12,000,000 to $15,000,000 in Alaska. Weighing this against the small population, one may think that Alaska has received unusually generous attention. However, when it is compared with the income produced in Alaska—approximately $100,000,000 a year—the amount hardly looks exorbitant; and even this is not an adequate way of appraising the expenditure, for Alaska's development as well as its welfare is (or should be) a national responsibility. In view of the size of the strategic region and the wealth of its still untapped resources, the sums appropriated for Alaska look like little more than token amounts.

Take, for example, the discovery of Alaska's minerals. Federal encouragement to prospectors has been almost non-existent. What little has been done along these lines has been done by the Territory itself.

While funds are now vastly increased under pressure of the war, in normal years the Geological Survey, which does the basic exploration work in Alaska, received an annual appropriation of only $60,000. Yet it had 586,400 square miles to cover. The amount was so small that, according to Dr. Philip Smith, Chief Alaskan Geologist, it was impossible for him to maintain a trained staff in the Territory. "We don't seem to have an enduring enough organization of law-makers," Dr. Smith told me. "There is still a disposition to regard Alaska as a barren iceberg."

Although work is now proceeding at a rapid pace, funds for the topographic mapping of the Territory have also been scant. At the time the war began the Survey had mapped less than a tenth of Alaska in detail and less than half of it even on an exploratory or reconnaissance basis. Long stretches of the rugged coastline had been left unexplored by the Coast and Geodetic Survey which was also handicapped by lack of funds.

Although the appropriation for the Alaska work of the Office of Indian Affairs, averaging between $2,000,000 and $2,500,000 a year, is one of the largest received by any agency in the Territory, it does not begin to meet the needs of the native population. Despite the high incidence of tuberculosis among the natives, there are only fifty-one beds available for those patients. While the number of beds has trebled under the New Deal Administration, it is still shamefully inadequate. According to one Indian Affairs official, at least a thousand beds are needed. In addition, the government has failed to extend to the Territory the community rehabilitation features of the Indian Reorganization Act of 1937, and consequently the Indian Affairs Office in Alaska receives funds for hospitals but no appropriations with which to build sewers or to tear down the crowded native villages where unsanitary living conditions are breeding the disease.

There has been no phase of our neglect of Alaska more important than our failure to provide it with roads. Despite their quarrels on many other matters, Alaska's business and government leaders are in agreement that more roads are a major essential to its future growth.

According to the Alaska Counselor to the National Resources Planning Board: "Alaska's poor road system is one of the chief reasons for its slow economic development."

According to Cap Lathrop: "The bottom of the whole story is roads. As soon as you put roads in, *pronto*, the industries and mines will spring up and take care of themselves."

The Federal Highway Act has not been extended to the Territory, and road funds, compared with those granted in the States, have been niggardly. They have hardly sufficed for maintenance—let alone new construction. There are still only a little over 2,500 miles of road in the entire region, or 23 lineal feet per square mile. This, as the Alaskans like to put it, is "hardly enough to turn a car around in." Most is low grade. Mr. William Hesse, Territorial Highway Engineer, has proposed a road program for the region which is heartily endorsed by most Alaskans. By adding some 1,000 miles of links and branches to existing roads, Mr. Hesse's scheme would give the region an "arterial" system of 2,100 connected miles, opening up many promising mineral and agricultural and scenic regions. Today, construction must proceed only according to military requirement, but a road network of this kind is considered a first essential in any development program for Alaska after the war.

A thoroughgoing development program is something that we have never had for our northern Territory, and the con-

trast between Alaska and the Soviet Arctic and Far East
regions is hardly flattering to the American record.

Alaskan aviators have great respect for the Russians' pioneer
achievements in Arctic aviation; for their daring transpolar
hops and their use of reconnnoitering planes along with
powerful ice-cutters to keep open the new commercial sea
route around the top of Siberia.

Weather Bureau officials in Alaska have long been envious
of the funds allotted to meteorological development on the
other side of the Strait. According to Mr. H. L. Thompson,
Meteorologist in charge of the Weather Bureau's main station in Alaska, the Russians have an enormous number of
Siberian stations. It is reported that the annual Soviet expendi-
ture for these stations runs into the millions, as compared
with the meager sum normally allotted to the Weather
Bureau in Alaska—usually less than $40,000. They are all
far superior to the makeshift affairs on which we depended
until the recent war program. Even at strategic Attu, our
most westerly Aleutian island, we had nothing but the simplest
kind of apparatus, tended by the husband of an Indian
Affairs schoolteacher. But, as described by Dr. Stefansson in
Alaska Life, a Soviet station like the ones at Wrangell and
Rudolf islands, "might have as much as a dozen scientists—
magneticians, zoologists, oceanographers, parasitologists, bot-
anists, and the like. Some of the stations have one or more
airplanes for upper air observations, for scouting to observe
ice movements and for communications with other stations."

Dr. Stefansson recently stated in the Department of Agriculture Yearbook:

During the last ten years, Soviet Arctic shipping has increased
many thousand percent. The population of several Arctic and sub-
Arctic towns has increased several hundred and even thousand
percent. The Archangel population figures are 76,774 for 1926

and 281,091 for 1939, an increase of 266.1%, the corresponding figures for Murmansk are 8,777 and 117,054 which is 1233.6% in thirteen years. Such is the growth of the places that were already cities. Where villages are grown to cities, the percentages are frequently colossal.

A few years ago he told a group of reporters, "The Russian colonization is far ahead of ours in almost every way. It's time we got busy."

While there are gold mines and salmon canneries in Alaska, and a few small sawmills, there is not one large manufacturing plant in the Territory. While the vast Soviet Far East is also for the most part undeveloped, already, in regions with climate similar to that of subarctic Alaska, it has huge factories producing aircraft motors, locomotives, railroad cars, mining machinery, and agricultural implements. While Alaska must import all its oil requirements, the Soviets have developed Siberian oil wells and have large refineries in operation. Three Soviet Far East cities—Komsomolsk, Khabarovsk and Ulan-Ude—have a combined population eight times that of all Alaska.

Regional Forester Frank Heintzleman also has admiration for Soviet accomplishment in Siberia. Mr. Heintzleman, who has been trying for over ten years to interest American businessmen in Alaska's spruce and hemlock forests, knows that a thriving lumber industry has been developed over in Siberia in the same period. The Arctic town of Igarka, for example, which had a population of only 500 ten years ago, has grown rapidly with that industry, and today it has a population of over 15,000.

Discussing the possibilities for Alaskan agriculture Dr. Bunnell, President of the University of Alaska, told me, "It's not the land that's the trouble. It's marketing difficulties. We could learn a lot from Russia."

According to James Rettie, Alaska Counselor of the National Resources Planning Board: "While the Russians may have spent more money than can be justified from a hard-headed point of view, they have developed a program which includes all the essentials—technical, economic, and social. In our own way, we should do the same thing for Alaska."

Today the war program is rapidly transforming Alaska, and for the first time the Territory is beginning to catch up with its northern neighbor. At last, under the threat of death and destruction, the United States is providing Alaska with fortifications and with facilities long needed in time of peace. Congress has appropriated a sum twenty-five times as large as the region's purchase price, and this time there is no argument about it. Now there is purpose and hope, and a willingness to spend far more. Titanic changes are being effected. The sourdoughs, the new Alaskans, even the soldiers feel it.

Writing at Fort Greely a few weeks after the Pearl Harbor attack, one of the editors of the Kodiak *Bear* declared in a lead editorial:

Something big is happening to Alaska—and we don't mean war.

It is doubtful if Alaskans, who have seen exciting times before, half appreciate what is taking place.

It is doubtful if they foresee the new economic and social pattern being shaped for this tremendous Territory by Uncle Sam's army of defense.

Alaska—America's big-boned, hard-fighting, gold-seeking, bear-tracking son, with the clear eyes, the lust for living and the sugar-bowl haircut—is growing up.

And fast!

The most significant advance is in transportation. Lack of transportation facilities both within Alaska and between Alaska and the States has been a basic obstacle to its development in the past. The new facilities now being provided will have enormous effects in the future. No longer will Alaska be a remote island. And even the new overland connection seems less important than other facilities now being provided—namely, the new network of large airports and air fields, weather stations, and aids to modern flying. It has taken a long time for Alaska to be made accessible to the States by land—now, simultaneously it is being made accessible by air to major centers of the civilized world.

Inside Alaska other transport facilities are being provided—facilities that have been sought for a long time by the people who live and work there. At last, as a result of Army pressure, a highway link is being built which will make it possible for the first time to drive between the two major inland towns; and other roads are projected. At last an ice-free port is being provided on Prince William Sound which will speed the rail service to the Interior. Additional buoys and markers are being installed along the rugged coasts and new lighthouses are flashing in the dark to guide our ships along the treacherous narrow channels.

On the economic front, too, Alaska is stirring in many ways under war's impact—as increased funds are provided for the development of strategic minerals, spruce for trainer planes is cut from the forests, and the output of the Matanuska farm colony is stepped up. Although a thoroughgoing program for economic development must wait till after the war, military necessity may develop Alaskan resources in other ways as the conflict continues.

The Territory's government structure is also improving under war necessity. Just as I finished this chapter, the President set up an Alaska War Council headed by the Governor to coordinate the work of leading federal officials in the Territory so that they may render more efficient support to the fighting forces. It is expected that this sensible step, long advocated in time of peace, will make some progress in eliminating the delays and confusions of the past. It provides that the designated officials in Alaska shall be invested by their superiors in Washington "with authority and responsibility as their representatives for making decisions requisite to the prompt performance of . . . duties and . . . to meeting emergencies requiring . . . special services." It is to be hoped that this is only one of many steps that our government may now take to strengthen Alaska into a more powerful instrument of war.

Many changes are being effected for Alaska today—and many more must occur as the war goes on, for the global character of the conflict has suddenly transformed the Territory from a remote byway into one of the most fateful crossroads of the entire war world. On the United States there lies a momentous responsibility for the region it bought so casually and managed so haphazardly down the years. A wartime plan and a policy for Alaska is a necessity, not only for the United States, but for the cause of all the United Nations. War is changing the history of Alaska. And in its turn, the region's strategic power may help change the course of the war.

The events of today lend some hope that the era of well-meaning planlessness for Alaska is a thing of the past—that Alaska will be fully strengthened and utilized in this war, and that in future years of peace it will come completely into its own, accorded recognition as a powerful, magnificent country.

As Vice President Wallace declared in his great Victory speech: "We failed in our job after World War I . . . But by our very errors we learned much, and after this war we shall be in a position to utilize our knowledge in building a world which is economically, politically, and . . . spiritually sound."

INDEX

fisheries, 168
fishing operations, Japanese, 14
fog, 68–71
food shortages, 99
forest fires, 186, 187
Forest Service, 158
Fort Nelson airfield, 82
Fort Richardson, 9, 38, 185
Fort St. John airfield, 82
Foster, Bud, 117
Fox Island, 11
freight rates, 152–5. *See also* transportation

Galena, 72
Gambell, 16
game, 92
Geist, Otto, 142
Geological Survey, 158, 187
German espionage, 17, 18
Gillam, Harold, pilot, 124
Goding, Wilfred, 34
gold mining, *see* mining
Gold Rush, 177, 180
Goodnews Bay platinum mine, 126
Gromov, Mikhail, Soviet aviator, 24
government, 150 ff.; history of, 179, 180
governor, powers of, 163, 164
Great Circle route, 12
Gruening, Ernest, Governor, 32, 80, 96, 98, 130, 163–176, 182
Gruening, Mrs. Ernest, 165–167
Guggenheim interests, 90

Hajdukovich, John, 161
harbor facilities, 193
Harriman, E. H., 22, 75, 76
Harris, P. E., 96
Heintzleman, B. Frank, 158, 186, 191
Hermann, Mildred, 175
Hesse, William, 189
Hiebert, August, 112–14
Highway, International, 21, 75–85
history, 180

home rule, 148, 149
Hoover, and International Highway, 77
Hoppin, Marshall, 64, 71, 72, 74
hospitals, 162, 170
Hughes, Howard, 60

Ickes, Harold, 106, 141–47, 161, 162, 182
Igarka, 191
Imports, 99
Indian Affairs, Office of, 161, 162, 189
Indian Reorganization Act, 162, 189
Indians, life of, 107, 117, 161, 162
industries, Alaskan, 123. *See also* fisheries, mining, agriculture
Interior, Department of, 151–56
International Highway, 21, 75–85
International Highway Association, 77
International Highway Commission, 80, 83
Ipiutak, 142

Jackson, Capt. E., 15
Japan, distance from Alaska, 11; interest in Alaskan affairs, 9, 75
Japan Current, 94
Japanese operations in Alaska, 14–17
Japanese residents, 16
Jefford, Jack, pilot, 63
Johann, A. E., 18
Johnson, Louis, 79
Jones, Jesse, 182
Joyce, Mary, 120
Juneau, 17, 59, 69, 150, 151
Juneau Women's Club, 175

Kamchatka, 28
Katella oil wells, 100
Kenai Peninsula, 92
Kennecott Copper Mines, 90
Ketchikan, 42, 60
Khabarovsk, 191

21

Crown Zellerbach

22-23

33
93
103

100

NORTH

Arctic Circle

U.

S.

S.   R.

2375

Irkutsk

Yakutsk

950

MANCHURIA

Khabarovsk

Markovo

Vladivostok

Anadyr

Sea

of Japan

re

915

Sea   of

Okhotsk

Sakhalin

Paramushiro

KAMCHATKA

Petropavlovsk

3510

Komandorskie
Is.

Bering

Kurile Islands

2000

Attu

850

Tokyo

Kiska

JAPAN

Aleutian

P   a   c   i   f   i   c

2000

Midway

STATUTE MILES

1200

Wake

0   500   1,000

NORTH - POLAR AZIMUTHAL
EQUIDISTANT PROJECTION